Praises

"*From Here to Serenity,* serves as a guide to overcome hardships that we face daily."

— Dexter E. Turner, MSCP/CSEE/CPMM,
Philips Healthcare, Director of Multi-Vendor Services

"The book rocks. Very pithy, true, and applicable. Good mix of practical insight with stories and example to root it into the brain/emotions. For me, it's a must read for everyone to understand how our internal software works and what we can do to upgrade it. It's college Psych 101 in a language you can understand, apply, and benefit from."

— Andy Christiansen, author of *The 40:40 Principle* and
President of High Capacity Leaders, LLC

"If you are wondering why you are stuck in destructive self-sabotaging cycles and are searching for inner peace and healing, then you should read this book. This is a book I will strongly recommend to all of my clients and families. Ed Clark explains the role of our past pain, and the core beliefs that stem from that and the resulting dysfunction in our lives today. This book brings an awareness to the present that not only helps you understand patterns, but also the path to true serenity."

— Kimberly Castro Owens, MSCM, Executive Director,
Recovery Outfitters Inc.

From Here
to Serenity

From Here
to Serenity

*Unraveling the Mysteries of Yesterday
and Today for a Better Tomorrow*

Edward Clark Jr., LPC, CCADC

**BOOK**LOGIX®
Alpharetta, Georgia

Copyright © 2013 by Life Focus, Inc.

ISBN: 978-1-61005-284-9
Library of Congress Control Number: 2012922194

Printed in the United States of America

♾This paper meets the requirements of ANSI/NISO Z39.48-1992 (Permanence of Paper)

Disclaimer: The names of former clients and any identifiable information or remarks have been altered in order to maintain confidential and privacy.

For bulk orders and to contact the author for lectures and speaking engagements, please contact: www.lifefocus.biz

Table of Contents

Preface

Several years ago, I was compelled to ask myself hard questions about the state of my heart and the condition of my relationships. I asked myself if I was willing to receive difficult answers so that I could better understand who I was and how I came to be the man I am today. I realized that I must first open myself to God's Will. It was this surrendering, giving up my perceived "control," expectations, and wants for what He wanted for me and trusting how He plans to get me there. The result was finding the answers to questions that plagued me for years.

According to the Apostle John:

> "It was God who gave me the truth of who I am: But when He, the Spirit of truth, comes, He will guide you into all truth. He will not speak on His own; He will speak only what He hears, and He will tell you what is yet to come."
>
> – 1 John 16:13

In opening my heart and mind to God's truth, I was unknowingly preparing myself to receive the answers to many questions. Throughout my transformation, He promised to comfort me through the pain of self-discovery and the hardships that accompany a mortal existence.

The old saying, "you don't get something for nothing" could not be truer when going through this process of transformation. It *will* cost you in time, sacrifice, discomfort, self-doubt, and disappointment. Without question, this was one of the most difficult processes I had ever experienced, but in the end, the pain of this process pales in comparison to what I eventually gained.

By making a commitment to this process, you will discover the real sources that lead to addictions, physical ailments, depression, anxiety, toxic relationships, and sexual immoralities. You will also learn about the kaleidoscope of past hurts and fears that we kept hidden, which leaves us in a constant state of apprehension, fear, and emotionally illiterate.

I entitled this book *From Here to Serenity* because of my developing concern for humanity's most common and dangerous issue, the issue of misunderstanding, as well as my belief that a positive and progressive transformation is not only possible, but assured to us according to the Word of God.

I pray this book helps to provide direction, motivation, answers, and an inner willingness to attain what few others have: knowledge, understanding and acceptance of self, and an understanding of how unique and loved you are by God.

Acknowledgments

In the course of writing this book, I truly appreciate those persons who have helped me along the way. It is by the grace of God, the situations, people, and events—both past and present—and the questions I asked myself that drove me to gain the answers that have brought me to a place of acceptance and fulfillment in my life. I also write this book in dedication to past, present and future clients. I am privileged to be an instrument of God, to serve them to the best of my ability; I learn just as much about myself as they learn from me.

I'd like to thank Melanie and Lance Henson, LPCs; Joseph Stapp, LPC; Christy Jones, PsyD, for their guidance on the art of counseling and insightful feedback. To Charles "Skeet" Stokes, MFT, for his patience, instruction, and wisdom. You have propelled me further than you will ever know. And to Roy Blankenship, LMFT, a counselor of impeccable skills.

To North Point Community Church, your environments and teachings have opened the eyes of my mind and heart toward God. To Dee Worley for her input and literary guidance, her efforts have helped me immensely in bringing this book's concepts and message into focus.

To my small groups both past and present, you have helped me connect to God; you have enriched my life. Thank you.

Last but certainly not least, to my beautiful wife Rochelle: Thank you for your love, honesty, support and patience, as well as sharing this journey called life with me. To Allana and Stephen who have shown me both the challenges and glories of what fatherhood is all about. To my children, may all of what I've become and gone through guide and assist you for many years to come. I could not have done it without you. I love you.

Introduction

"Choosing not to change or choosing to change are one in the same; both are decisions requiring the same amount of effort to achieve, but with drastically different results."

– Edward Clark

"Like a dog that returns to its' vomit, so is a fool who repeats his folly."

– Proverbs 26:11

I am not going to sugarcoat this process. My ongoing personal journey toward spiritual maturity, emotional balance, inner peace, and clarity of mind has been, at times, a very painful, tedious and uncomfortable. However, it has also been an equally rewarding, confidence building, and an insightful journey.

You will learn it takes a combination of self-reflection, awareness and courage to see who you truly are without substituting it for an easily accessible public face or false self. Likewise, as you begin your journey, you will see the real you, your strengths, weaknesses, neediness, and the gifts given to you by God will be unveiled. In this book, you will see the masks others wear for the same reasons you wear your own. This self-understanding will forever change your current impression of God, and how you relate to others.

The purpose of this book is to help you gain more awareness of how you address the issues of today, how you currently interfere with addressing those issues and to consider how the painful experiences of your past can assist in your healing. You will understand the various ways pain is avoided and how this avoidance inhibits the process of healing from those pains. We will examine how we fall into Satan's traps and how we trap others in deceit and manipulation. You will learn how God uses relationships for healing and how the gift of relationships is leveraged by God to deliver us from our pain into the serenity of peace and restoration.

Reading this book and answering the questions at the end of each chapter, as well as doing the exercises in the appendix section, will spark new questions, which will take you to the answers you seek, or to surprisingly new directions and insights.

With courage and persistence to address these questions with boldness and wisdom, we will gradually leave our old selves behind, while gaining confidence in your new selves.

There is no one question, specific timetable, or medication that will speed up this process. Every stage of life, every uncomfortable childhood memory, or significant relationship you had must be diligently reviewed, taken apart and addressed before being able to move forward taking on age appropriate responsibilities and tasks.

If you are not committed to this journey or are applying the bare minimum of effort in this process, it should be no surprise if you are still trapped in your self-doubt, confusion, chaotic relationships, addictions, and continue to make poor decisions. The effort you apply is proportional to the results you receive! The choice is yours. Since you are reading this book, I assume you have decided and are motivated to find your uniqueness within these pages. As in any journey, there are great insights and discoveries to be made. Take your time, but most importantly, stay committed and optimistic in your journey, receiving the blessings God is revealing to you.

1

My Own Worst Enemy

"The mind is its own place, and in itself,
can make a Heaven of Hell and a Hell of Heaven."

– John Milton

"To step out of our own way is often the first step
in seeing the path laid out before us."

– Edward Clark

In this chapter, we will discuss the reasons why we sabotage our healing efforts and the various obstacles in becoming self-aware. We will determine what we must do to overcome this deficiency, and see what the Word of God says about this plight.

Each one of us sees the world in our own particular way. We see the world through the filter of our own experiences, triumphs, and tragedies. We are comfortable with our viewpoints, they're familiar and predictable. When other beliefs or circumstances go against how we envision reality or what we want. We become defensive, even hostile, toward those whose beliefs and ideologies contradict our own.

We tend to see our view as right and everyone else as wrong or misguided. We are our own worst enemy because we struggle to see other points of view, ideologies, and beliefs other than our own, often, narrow minded and skewed vantage point. Often, we want to continue seeing life as it *appears* to be, fearful of what we may discover about ourselves or others we love. Often, we are so stuck in how we see the world that we will fight to maintain it. Some will even defend their view through extreme methods including murder. For instance, most people are hesitant to talk about their childhood or how their parents parented them. There is a fear of shattering their current view or idea about their parents. This brings resistance in looking at a crucial part of development. This blind spot (which we will discuss later in the book) can cause significant problems well into adulthood.

It is easier to question others' views rather than our own. The problems with overlooking ourselves and focusing elsewhere are: 1) we lack ability and confidence to assess our own life circumstances accurately and appropriately. We will continuously reach the wrong conclusions; thus, making poor choices based on poor conclusions. 2) We avoid taking responsibility for the condition of our life. We stay the victim, constantly looking outside of ourselves for help or for someone to blame. This perpetuates dependency on others and low self-esteem.

Most people seldom, if ever, challenge their way of seeing themselves, others, or life in general. Even fewer ask themselves questions about what they have experienced, how they have been affected by their experiences, and how they are coping or reacting to those experiences. In order to start getting out of our own way, we must take the initiative in questioning how we see the current condition of our lives. I believe we must first stop asking others these critical questions, insisting that they change their ways, and instead pose these kinds of questions to ourselves. Some examples of inward directed questions are:

- How does this situation, event or person make me feel?
- How does this situation, event or person affect how I view myself?
- How does my handling of the situation impact others?
- What is the appropriate way to handle this situation?

If questions like these go unasked or unanswered prior to times of conflict, loneliness, and stressful situations, we can quickly feel an overwhelming sense of helplessness and powerlessness. This lack of self-reflection is often accompanied by negative emotions of ourselves that we project onto others in order to avoid how we feel. We blame-shift or judge others as a way to rationalize our way of perceiving things as correct and others perceived as flawed. For instance, there are a number of talent shows on television where contestants audition for a spot on the show. Many contestants are eliminated and feel sad, disappointed or hurt, some feel grateful for the opportunity and decide to take the advice of the judges and try again next time. However, there are some who believe they are more talented then they truly are.

When the reality of the judges' assessment and not being chosen meet the fantasy of the contestant, these contestants are more than hurt, they are angry because their expectations, assumptions, and views are drastically different than reality. The judges' assessments conflict with the contestants' viewpoint of themselves. These contestants reject a view that opposes their own, they will stomp off stage, arguing, pleading or cussing at the judges. The contestants leave still believing that others are mistaken or they are the victims of unfairness.

Unfortunately, most people have very little understanding of who they are or why they do what they do. It is essential to know why we act, think, believe and feel the way we do. When we say, "It's him/her," instead of asking "Is it me," we miss opportunities to adjust or change our distorted beliefs or misperceptions that are often the root cause in poor decision-making.

There are three main reasons why we sabotage our ability to see ourselves:

1. Our technological inventions have altered how we interact with one another.

The more we integrate new social media—such as: blogging, emails, texting, Facebook, MySpace, Twitter, Blackberry, iPhones, and so on—the more distant from one another we become, the more we risk becoming strangers to ourselves and skeptical of others. These types of social networking environments are taking the place of face-to-face intimate socializing encounters.

The present iGeneration are losing their ability to effectively pick up on social cues that are acquired in face-to-face conversations; this relational disconnection often results in more misunderstandings and an increase in dysfunctional relationships. It has become apparent—particularly in adolescents and young adults—that they are lacking crucial intrapersonal skills needed to explore, identify, and express themselves appropriately. The phenomenon of cyber-bullying is a good example of this. It teaches kids they don't have to talk out their problems, face their fears, or learn real resolution skills. This gives kids a way out of solving conflicts face-to-face and retards emotional development. With our increasing dependency on technology, we are more reliant on these devices, rather than genuinely vocalizing our deeper inner selves to one another.

The lack of face-to-face encounters and the resulting negative impact on seeing ourselves objectively cannot be emphasized enough. Face-to-face conversations give us relational feedback on ourselves that we cannot get from any device. This feedback enables us to readjust our tone, body language, ideas, reevaluate our beliefs, and helps us to articulate our thoughts and feelings based on the emotional tone and facial expression shown during the encounter. Without intimate face-to-face dialog, we lose our ability to empathize with others, learning to shift our perspective, seeing their situation from their position instead of relying on our own perceptional lens. Having little to no daily face-to-face dialog, is like getting up every morning and not having a mirror to look at yourself before going to work. We would be guessing about how we really look.

According to technology-author Nicholas Carr:

> ...The very nature of the Internet, with all of its distractions and tendency to promote short, easy-to-find content, promotes surface thinking and discourages reflection, contemplation, and concentration. With the ever-increasing ubiquity of the Internet—which has become the primary medium for work, entertainment, socializing, and educational research —the result will be a radical shift in the very way we *think*...Over and over again studies show that children's brains develop best when there is actual interaction with an adult, especially in the area of language. When supported with frequent feedback, emotional support, and exposure to enriched environments, learning enhanced. Spending 'face-to-face' time with an adult reading, talking, walking, and interacting are all invaluable for brain development.

Our personal development is only gained by expressing inner struggles, discussing mutual problematic behaviors and attitudes. In face-to-face confrontation, both parties gain through hearing, seeing and emotionally experiencing themselves through the eyes of another.

2. The majority of our interests and focus is in an outward direction instead of self-reflection, which focuses on self-understanding and personal growth.

We would rather compare ourselves to others, focusing on what we have or don't have. Many people live vicariously through other people, and by focusing outside of ourselves, we ignore our present emotional, spiritual, and psychological condition that interferes with addressing our pain, which may be hidden in our unawareness. Therefore, our hurt remains unnoticed and the chronic dysfunction in our lives continues unabated. An excessive outward focus is what I call *self-abandonment*. For example: a celebrity's life takes center stage creating magazines and entertainment news shows; reality based television shows takes advantage of our insatiable appetite for drama, intrigue, and scandal. We will do anything not to live, look at or change our own lives. We are more judging and critical of other lives, relationships, and behaviors than our own. These public figures have become the targets for our focused judgments, interests, bias, and criticisms, as well as fantasies. As long as we have them, we can abandon ourselves for something better, leaving our dissatisfied lives behind, at least for the time being.

3. Self-examination is difficult because of our unique methods of self-protection.

Our conscious coping behaviors manifest as addictions: drugs, drinking, television, sex, etc. In addition, our unconscious defenses—such as: denial, rationalization, and projection (blaming or placing our emotions on others)—get in the way of our own ability to really see ourselves. These self-protective methods are helpful when we are experiencing overwhelming pain. However, if our defenses and coping behaviors are overused, these once defenders now become the hunters and we their prey. This is similar to our body's immune response where the body attempts to defend itself from attacking invaders. In the case of autoimmune disorders, the body mistakenly believes it is the foreign invader, attacking itself.

In essence, we go into a similar reaction when we attempt our own emotional, psychological, spiritual self-examination. Our defenses see this self-reflection as a foreign invader; inquires and challenges are seen as the enemy. Ironically, the very protection we rely on to get us through—or to minimize the trauma, pain and grief we experience in life—is the same protection that restricts us from dealing with the pain and hurt that is sabotaging our efforts at recovery and healing.

If our inner-self and the pain of our past and present hurts remains misunderstood, numbed by substances or purposefully hidden out of view, our dysfunctional inner-self *will* sabotage any future plans, desires, wants or successes no matter how well-intentioned we may be.

Joe's Story

A former client of mine (we will call him Joe), grew up with an alcoholic father who celebrated everything by drinking. One day when Joe received a notice from his boss that he would be getting a promotion and a raise, he decided to celebrate. What were Joe's choices? He could have chosen not to drink (vowing never to be like his father) or he may do exactly what his father did and drink to his success. Unfortunately, Joe chose the latter and drank too much at a local bar with some co-workers. He quickly lost control of his actions and began to behave inappropriately with a female co-worker. He left the bar and got arrested for driving under the influence. The consequences of Joe's behavior were that his promotion was taken away, he lost the respect of his co-workers, and his job was in jeopardy.

Like many clients I have counseled, Joe's past hurtful childhood experiences became an unconscious influence on his present behaviors. It is this lack of self-reflection and self-awareness that contributes to his inability to connect his past experiences to his present behaviors that enslave Joe and bring about negative consequences. He, like many others, hates the way he presently acts. Frequently I hear clients' say, "I don't understand why I behave, think, or feel this way…" And, "I have tried many times to stop my behaviors, but they continue…"

By accepting responsibility for your life condition and the condition of your relationships, (this takes self-reflection) you take the first step toward lasting change. The Word is very clear on taking responsibly and being accountable for our lives. According to Matthew 7:3-5:

> "Why do you look at the speck of sawdust in your brother's eye and pay no attention to the plank in your own eye? How can you say to your brother, 'Let me take the speck out of your eye,' when all the time there is a plank in your own eye? You hypocrite, first take the plank out of your own eye, and then you will see clearly to remove the speck from your brother's eye."

Without self-understanding, reflection, and awareness, we are doomed to repeat the same unhealthy behaviors, thoughts and overwhelming feelings of the past. We will receive the same results when we keep the same views, perspectives and beliefs. We are either like puppets being controlled by our emotional, psychological strings (baggage) or we are in the role of a puppeteer, in need of controlling others' lives to fulfill our own lives. We find ourselves performing in situations we do not like; afraid to stop performing for fear of how others will react, or of possibly not being accepted by others. We continue the performance no matter how destructive or shameful the behaviors may be. We are dependent on our behaviors, views and beliefs about our world because it is all we know.

Tools to Use

Here are some practical ways to get out of your own way and start healing:

1. Realize your internal resistance to see yourself clearly and objectively due to your own defense mechanisms and coping strategies.
2. Challenge your views or beliefs by asking yourself inward directed questions (like the ones at the end of the chapter).
3. Ask five trusted friends and family members:
   a. "How am I sabotaging my recovery efforts?"
   b. "What is it about me that concerns you?"
   c. "What are my strengths?"
   d. In your opinion, "Am I open to change?"
4. Start a daily journal *immediately* in order to document your thoughts, feelings and ways you dealt with daily stressors, relationships and events. Journaling is an excellent way to bring your inner self to life (in words), this will help you in reflecting on how you see yourself and situations, instead of keeping it in your head where it is more likely to be skewed, rationalized and forgotten before any changes can take place.

5. It is important to understand that permanent change is a gradual process involving small but consistent steps that alter harmful behaviors, perceptions, beliefs and so on. The brain cannot make big changes quickly or changes that contradict what you truly believe. (For instance, you may want to stop using drugs, but if you believe "I am unworthy or inadequate" you will continue to use drugs to cope with life stressors, because you internally believe you

are not able to handle the stressors.) *Our Core beliefs will ultimately override our conscious intentions, desires and wants.*

Key Points

The choice is yours. You can either:

1. Choose to avoid, numb, or detach yourself from the reality of your current condition, hoping that the condition or circumstance will somehow "work itself out" with little or no effort by you, or hopefully someone such as a parent or someone you are dependent on will come and save you.

2. You can ask God to help you to come to terms with your current life issues and struggles through self-reflection and time in prayer. To bring healthy people into your life that will speak truth to you and for strength to receive that truth.

One of the above choices does bring instant relief, but a lifetime of misery and continued avoidance of real issues. The other choice, brings immediate discomfort and pain, but a lifetime of positive, productive living, and close relationships. The latter choice is characteristic of self-understanding and awareness, which we will discuss in greater detail in the next chapter.

Take *your time* in reflecting on the questions, and allow yourself to experience the feelings that may come from the questions, memories, or answers that are revealed. *For group discussions,* the group facilitator should allow group members to discuss their answers, thoughts, and feelings as well as permitting appropriate feedback from other group members.

Questions to Ponder

1. What are some difficult topics for you to talk about?
2. What are your thoughts and feelings about Chapter 1?
3. What was your childhood like? Describe it in 200 words or less.
4. How do you presently see God in your life?
5. What is it about yourself you are most afraid for others to know?
6. How do you distract others from knowing you better?
7. How do you generally cope with pain and hurt?
8. How do you deceive yourself?
9. How do you resist change?
10. List five advantages to changing.
11. List five disadvantages to changing. (Yes, there are disadvantages.)
12. Which traumatic event in your life is likely to skew how you see yourself?
13. Are you defensive when asked to look at the viewpoints or beliefs of others?

2

The Enigmatic Self

"Self-analysis and reflection are man's granted gifts from God, so we can glimpse at our frailties and potentiality."

— Edward Clark

"We are drowning in information, but starved for Knowledge."

— John Naisbitt

As mentioned earlier, the importance of understanding ourselves cannot be over-emphasized. In this chapter, we will look at self-reflection and self-awareness in greater detail and how mastering these crucial skills will achieve self-understanding and peace.

We are bound to encounter challenging situations, difficult people, and the unexpected in life. Knowing *ourselves* is the goal, knowing who we truly are also equips us to handle these encounters in the healthiest way possible. The process must first begin with turning our attention inward, and spending time in self-reflection. One way to do this is by looking at the four areas illustrated by the Johari window diagram (seen below). The Johari window is an effective tool to better understand ourselves and others. The four windows are as follows:

- **Public self:** The part of you everyone knows and what you know about yourself, i.e. feelings, behaviors, thoughts, etc.

- **Blind Spot:** This area we are not aware of, but others see it, i.e. our denial and deceptive selves.

- **Hidden self:** This area we keep secret from others out of fear they may reject, judge or leave, i.e. addictions, intentions, personal information.

- **Unknown self:** This area is unknown to others and ourselves, i.e. unconscious aptitudes, repressed memories that drive our core beliefs and feelings.

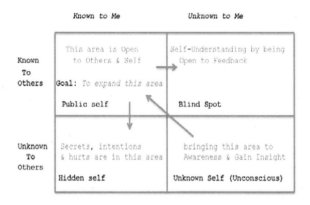

To gain self-understanding, we utilize tools such as the Johari window (above) to pinpoint areas of ourselves with the most influence, and what we store in those areas such as: perceptions, thoughts, feelings, beliefs, etc. It reveals and brings insight to how we respond to the world around us.

The Johari window also shows areas that may reveal our problematic areas. Self-reflecting and self-awareness are tools that, when used consistently, empower us by bringing aspects of ourselves that are problematic into awareness so that we may address them. Through self-reflection and awareness, we expose these problematic issues to the light of conscious understanding where insight occurs (bringing our darkness into the light of change), and action becomes a precursor to gaining manageability of our life.

Applying the Johari Window

The Johari window is an excellent way to reflect on particular areas of your life. First, on a sheet of paper, list any feedback you have received from others or have been told to you over the years. This is listed under the "Blind Spot." Under the Public Self area, list what you allow others to know about you. Do the same for the Hidden Self, the Unknown self. (Note: the Unknown Self, should be the last area you work on. Apply what you have learned from the other areas to help reveal what was once unknown to you.) The more effort and time applied to this exercise the better understanding is gained. Self-reflection and self-awareness are both action and insight modes that are of the utmost importance in the growth and maturity of character. Each represents the first steps toward healing.

What is self-reflection? I believe *self-reflection is the practice of focusing our attention in such a way that includes our observational, sensory, and intuitive skills in order to see how we engage, communicate, and connect our inner/outer selves to the world around us.* By engaging in self-reflection, we *first* learn to intentionally shift our concentration from exterior situations, events and relationships to how we are currently feeling (physically and emotionally), thinking and believing about current and past experiences. With practice, we will eventually acquire the ability to integrate how we see our inner self with our outer circumstances in order to give a proper response. For instance, if a friend disappoints us by not showing up for a date, with self-reflection we begin by asking ourselves the following questions:

What am I feeling right now? (Emotionally focused)

How am I behaving at this moment? (Behaviorally focused)

What do I think or believe about this situation? (Cognitively focused)

In self-reflection, we are consciously aware of the direction of our attention. With continued practice, we can develop our ability to turn our attention inward at any given time. There are three essential parts to self-reflection:

1) **Pre-reflection** involves reflecting on your thoughts, feelings, and beliefs *prior to the event, encounter or situation.* For instance, if you are going to encounter a stressful situation like being asked to meet with your boss regarding an important project you are responsible for, it is important to ask yourself the following questions:

   - Have I handled a situation like this in the past inappropriately?
   - What do I anticipate happening during this situation?
   - What is the best way to handle this situation appropriately?

2) **In-the-moment reflection** is reflecting on how you are *handling yourself during the event.* For example, if you are confronting a family member regarding their actions and how they have hurt you, you are reflecting on how you are expressing

yourself (emotions felt, body language, tone of voice, etc.) to them. Questions to ask ourselves are:

- Am I expressing myself clearly?
- What do I feel or think right now?
- Am I currently behaving inappropriately, in light of the current situation?

3) Post-reflection is the *self-evaluation/assessing of a past occurrence and how you handled the occurrence.* You would ask yourself the following:

- Did I handle the situation better than past similar situations?
- How are my feelings and beliefs about the situation different now, then before the situation happened?
- How could I have handle the situation or myself differently?

Self-reflection is a critical step toward self-understanding. Without reflecting on ourselves before, during, and after a situation, encounter, or event we lose valuable information and opportunities that can aid in our insight into how we can better apply and handle situations that are similar in the future. Therefore, we stop problematic attitudes, prejudices, and behaviors from repeating or becoming progressively worse.

Without self-reflection we remain hopelessly reactive—unable to respond to or understand how to adjust to the circumstances of life. We remain inhibited in our ability to adapt and to navigate through life effectively and lovingly. Self-reflection exposes secrecies, lies, powerlessness, and vulnerabilities to our awareness. From there we can address the various issues that are uncovered.

Self-awareness is the next stage reached after self-reflection has been mastered. *In the self-awareness stage, we are cognizant of—or bring to focused attention—our beliefs, values, emotionality, physical senses, and thoughts, etc. We experience our present feelings, thoughts, and are able to recognize how our actions and beliefs are affecting others and are being affected by others.*

In self-awareness, we become tuned in to how we are impacted by our own actions and decisions. By developing self-awareness, we are better equipped and confident in how we respond to life's diverse encounters, situations, and the ups and downs of everyday relationships.

Self-awareness not only trains us to pay attention to our fundamental components such as our emotions, perceptions, beliefs, behaviors and so on. In addition, self-awareness development allows us the ability to change how we perceive, interpret, or dispute messages, views, and/or opinions we receive from the outside world.

Imagine a person struggling with the pain of an inner conflict. Add to that struggle being unaware of it, what's causing it and finally, how to stop it. Like many of us, this person is likely to learn how to cope with *it by using past coping behaviors like drugs, sex, isolation,* or other means to minimize the pain of their inner conflict. For instance, ever since she was a child, a young woman had unresolved hurt and feeling neglected by her workaholic father. She numbs her pain with heroin and uses sexually promiscuous behaviors to gain temporary feelings of affection and validation from men. Like this young woman, people are convinced they are fundamentally flawed, inadequate and unworthy and develop the belief of "That's just the way I am."

With the understanding of both self-reflection and awareness, as well as applying the tools in this book, we can challenge our old views, behaviors, and beliefs against our newly acquired understandings and truth; thus enabling us to respond effectively, adapting in appropriate ways to whatever we encounter.

In evaluating and comparing our current behaviors, beliefs and perceptions to our internal standards and values, we become self-aware, which moves us in the direction of maturity and restoration. I believe the measure of a person's unhealthiness or dysfunction comes from their inability to see themselves realistically, (the contrast between their "real self" and their "perceived self") and from their reluctance to spend quality time with themselves (solitude) without using some form of coping such as alcohol or drugs. *My reference to solitude does not include engaging in distracting activities such as television, video games, etc., but in purposeful, contemplative introspection.* An excellent example of purposeful solitude is spending quality time in prayer, looking to God's Word and taking God's Word and its meaning and integrating it into daily life.

The Gospels tell of Paul's undeniable faith in God because of the time he spent in quiet reflection (even while he was imprisoned in Rome). Through quality time with God, Paul became knowledgeable and acutely aware of Satan's schemes against the flesh. God's gift to humanity is the ability to look at ourselves and to receive from others about ourselves. God, through His Word, gives us wisdom and guidance from Satan's deceit and traps.

"Get wisdom, get understanding; do not forget my words or swerve from them. Do not forsake wisdom, and she will protect you. Wisdom is supreme; therefore get wisdom. Though it cost all you have, get understanding."

– Proverbs 4:5-7

Jesus applied these principles for us to follow. Self-reflection and self-awareness are God's gifts to us. By overlooking these gifts, we diminish our capacity to do His Will in seeing our true selves, seeing where we fit in God's grand plan and in accepting God's purpose for our lives. Self-awareness is simply the skill of seeing ourselves in the most realistic and elementary way. We must see ourselves first, before we can see and relate to others on multiple levels and at various points-of-view.

Bill's Story

"Bill" was a forty-two-year-old client of mine who battled alcohol abuse for most of his life. Bill's focus was more on being accepted by others and what they thought of him. Bill lacked the skill of seeing himself, and instead focused on the reactions of others as well as attempting to avoid unanticipated situations. All the while, Bill felt as if he was less than a man and fundamentally empty as a person. Bill was consumed by uncontested beliefs that he was "inadequate" compared to others.

As we started therapy, it became obvious that he lacked the skill to self-reflect, which pointed to his lack of awareness regarding his positive attributes and talents. Bill was also blind to how he was feeling about himself at any given moment. He struggled to identify his feelings and expressing them appropriately. Bill was unaware how daily situations affected him. He avoided social events and any situation that brought attention to himself.

Bill lacked the fundamental skill of capturing negative thoughts that consistently played in his mind like a broken record. Because of Bill's inability to shift his focus and gain awareness "to connect the dots," he became a slave to the outside world and a stranger to his internal self. This dissonance between reality and his distorted view of the world, brought about feelings of frustration and anger at himself for not being able to stop drinking, and self-hatred about himself and how he repeatedly disappointed his family and friends.

Bill's excessive focus outward and his inability to look inward were major contributors to his lack of insight about his drinking problem. His destructive behaviors only added to his negative self-image. Bill's therapy began with helping him understand the link between his childhood pain and the emotional deprivation he experienced, which led to his present condition.

We examined how he used alcohol and deceptive thinking to cope with his inner pain, current circumstances and emptiness. I assigned Bill exercises to strengthen his ability to direct his focused attention onto his thoughts, beliefs, and feelings.

Bill began to learn to experience emotions without having to avoid them out of fear. Over the process of counseling, Bill began to learn he could identify, experience and express his inner self with acceptance and peace. Bill is presently doing well and currently working on rebuilding the relationships his drinking damaged.

According to Bill, "the greatest lesson I learned from my ordeal is how utterly foolish it was to make the things of this world my idol…I made others my god and relied less on the one thing that could bring me true contentment; the Lord Jesus Christ." The Word of God says,

---

"Do not store up for yourselves treasures on earth, where moth and rust destroy, and where thieves break in and steal. But store up for yourselves treasures in heaven, where moth and rust do not destroy, and where thieves do not break in and steal. For where your treasure is there your heart will be also."
— Matthew 6:19-21

Tools to Use

Self-awareness and reflection are achieved through a variety of methods.

1. Quiet time in the Word; learning the nature of God and His message for righteous living.

2. Reading books on personal growth (particularly from a Christian perspective).

3. Take the time to answer the end of chapter questions.

4. Take time to focus on breathing and identifying current emotions being felt.

As we have discussed earlier, the steps on the path to recovery using self-reflection and self-awareness, will generally look like this:

1. A person generally experiences overwhelming external and or internal stresses; denial, fantasizing, drug abuse or other means of escape or deception can no longer hide/cope with the pain and suffering.

2. The pain and suffering forces the person to reevaluate their coping strategies. They realize their old coping ways are not able to divert the culmination of consequences and the reality that their dysfunctional life has become. This revelation brings about self-reflection onto both internal and external worlds, which can be a strong motivator to look at him or herself from an alternate perspective.

3. As self-reflection intensifies and it becomes more consistent, self-awareness increases, thereby increasing receptiveness to solutions.

4. Consistent self-awareness produces self-understanding, which results in:

   a. Problem identification,
   b. Realistic understanding of the impact the problems has on every area of life,
   c. Openness to learning and applying new solutions to identified problems.

5. When self-understanding is reached, we become more confident with an increased commitment to the process of achieving solutions by:

   a. Developing healthy support systems (healthy family, friends and community groups, etc.),
   b. Building knowledge and skills to minimize or eliminate the problems,
   c. Developing self-discipline and persistence in applying the solutions.

6. Recovery is the process of reaching self-acceptance of what has occurred in your past that includes:

   a. How you have been hurt, betrayed, abused, abandoned and so on by others?
   b. How you have hurt, betrayed, abused, or neglected others in your life?

Self-acceptance also means accepting where you presently are in your life and coming to terms with the poor and costly decisions that were made. It is looking from another's point of view as to the reason(s) why they no longer want a relationship with you.

Self-reflection and self-awareness bring an understanding that *You are not your behaviors!* Your behaviors are simply an action used to handle a situation. You (the person) are much more than a habit, reaction, or behavior. Self-acceptance is the understanding of your place in God's creation and not just among one of His creations

Key Point

As we reflect more on ourselves, we become more aware that something is off—out of balance. We are able to identify the chronic feeling of emptiness, sadness, or some other dissatisfaction with who we are and or where we are in life. We start realizing that we are capable of making needed changes. We begin to realize that all past attempts to see clearly, failed because we tried to change from the same point-of-view that got us in our current mess.

Truly the best gift anyone can give to him or herself is the gift of a healthy self-image, self-acceptance and knowledge of self. By committing to this study, the study of self and the methods of change, we gain a world anew—a fresh perspective of how influential important relationships are to us, and in return how we influence others by our actions, words, and beliefs.

As long as we consistently reflect on and bring into awareness our pain, hurts, and challenges through appropriate expression, our hidden suffering no longer remains a mystery to fear or to avoid. We will no longer remain slaves to their effects, nor will we remain slaves to a superficial mask, false personas, or to manipulative talk and behaviors that we conjure up to escape from our feelings and the scrutiny of others. If you are currently reading this book, then God is moving you in a direction of healing and growth. If you are not committed to healing now, then when will you be? The cost usually is much greater later than it is now.

Questions to Ponder

1. What are you feeling at this very moment?

2. Are you more interested in avoiding others or being accepted by others?
3. When you reflect on your life, how does this make you feel?
4. What event, situation or person in your past has affected you the most? And, how has it affected you?
5. What current issue(s) are the most challenging for you?
6. How do your behaviors and the people around you keep your issue(s) from being resolved?
7. What would need to happen for your situation or problem(s) to change for the better?

3

Origins of Ordeal

"The people you have around you; are sure signs of what's inside you."

— Edward Clark

"Without proper guidance, parents become the bones on which their children sharpen their teeth."

— Peter Ustinov

E ver since the Garden of Eden, man has struggled with inflicting suffering onto his brother. We lie, cheat, abuse, manipulate, hurt, kill...and so on. As unique creations of God, we are capable of many wondrous and loving acts. Because of our inherent sinful nature and the resulting separation from God, we start out life both innocent and needy; however, where we are in our current life circumstances often reveals the extent of sin hold in our life. It is imperative to examine how our sin nature has influenced the method(s) in which we are meeting those needs. In this chapter, we will discuss the role sin plays in our pain, neediness, and suffering, and how certain relationships, beliefs and thoughts can perpetuate our sinful behaviors and hurt. We will also explore how to understand the nature of

God's salvation and how it brings us into balance and harmony.

We are in a constant fight to overcome the temptations of this world. A world distorted in the notion that more is better, substances, fame, power and money are the things that encapsulate who we are and are relationship with God is only called forth when we are in need of His help in obtaining the "worldly things."

In order to understand our ordeal we must first understand the nature of sin and how it contaminates and eventually destroys our ability to make proper choices and have fulfilling relationships. Sin can be defined as a human brokenness or an inherited separation from God. Our ordeal resides in our reluctance to surrender our perceived "control" over to God.

It is in our ignorance of God's nature we fail to receive His salvation and forgiveness. It is our ignorance of our Heavenly Father that allows sinful deeds to go unabated and strengthen the enemy's foothold in our lives.

Our sinful nature is in partnership with our relentless quest to quench our neediness despite the injury it causes to others. It is this ordeal of sin and our need to selfishly gratify our desires that has us struggling with a variety of humanistic ailments, depravity and hurtful issues. This gratification of our flesh is a tactic of Satan. This tactic moves us away from inner authentic peace through the use of fear, self-doubt and mistrust. Satan uses our sin (tendency to separate from God) and fears (our feelings of shame, inadequacies and frailties) in various ways:

1. The enemy knows the insecurities within us, this keeps us afraid and anxious to self-reflect and fearful to engage in quiet time alone.
2. The enemy distorts how we see sin, we view sin from a victim and or slave mentality, pre-destined to

live in separation from God; unable to respond appropriately to the pain, desires and temptations as part of a mortal existence.

3. Sin develops in the weakness of character; when we are distracted by neediness and by the ignorance of its existence.

4. The enemy uses our hurt and pain to distort the true nature of God. Through this hurt, we view a God that possesses human frailties, such as: anger, vengefulness, indifference, heartlessness, and coldness.

The enemy leaves his footprint upon our soul through the daily echoing of negative beliefs, lies and thoughts regarding our relationship with God and others. We often entertain and rationalize the very pain, beliefs, sin, and struggles we have vowed to rid ourselves of.

> "Then, after desire has conceived, it gives birth to sin; and sin, when it is full-grown, gives birth to death."
>
> — James 1:15

Sin assumes many forms, and similar to restoration, sin's growth is a process. It inflicts us individually and subtly saturates the very culture some of us idolize. We have not just succumbed to its influence and devastating effects, but we have also begun to minimize and even rationalize sin and its influence on behaviors and beliefs (i.e. cultural and political submission to materialism, moral and sexual deviancies, alternate family structure, and so on).

The origin of our ordeal is also found in the enemy's edict that we are our behaviors. *It is vital that we distinguish that we are not our behaviors. Yes, our behaviors do say something about us, our past experiences and what we are trying to achieve, but this is very different than to say we ARE our behaviors.* Our sin and its manifested behaviors are symptoms of a much deeper issue. It is a mistake to label ourselves and judge others simply based on the behaviors. The Word is clear on this point.

> "Do not judge or you too will be judged. For in the same way you judge others, you will be judged, and with the measure you use, it will be measured to you."
>
> – Matthew 7:1-2

Imagine if a person stumbles out of the desert on the verge of death from thirst, and comes across a food stand with cold bottled water. He grabs the water and drinks it. Is he a thief? Or has he stolen? A thief is a person who has a consistent habit or behavior of stealing. The person in the above scenario stole in a desperate act to get his need met (thirst). Perhaps this is an action out of need (survival) and not so much a want (desire).

Most of us do the former. We act out of need and before we know it, if we are not careful, we label ourselves based on the action. *We end up believing we are our sinful behaviors, and forget the neediness that drives them.*

It is in our early childhood environments that are the very breeding ground for the development and spreading of sin. Sin, like a virus, attaches, grows in the host and spreads from family member to family member, then attaches to other families and on to whole communities.

Sin is not confined by time, it moves from one generation to another. Sin is so pervasive it conceals itself as part of "pop" culture or popular fads i.e. sinful behaviors or attitudes in media such as *American Idol* (the name says it all) and *The New Normal Show* are distorted views of values and priorities.

These deviancies and distortions are constantly marketed and push onto the public in order to be accepted and integrated into our lives. When culture starts endorsing this behavior, it should be no surprise that sharp increases in children born out of wedlock, personal debt ("keeping up with the Joneses"), crime, addiction, etc. occur. This societal acceptance of sin is a major contributing factor to the increase of single mothers and absent fathers, which is just one component in an ever-increasing problem of dysfunctional homes and families. But make no mistake—sin can and will disguise itself as something better than what it truly is.

Even with the best intentions and motives, parents and families are no exception to the wicked behaviors, self-serving nature, and drive of a sinful nature. As adults, we must understand, examine, and accept how our childhood families—our first classroom—really operated and how we learned to relate to others within that environment.

Roles within Relationships

Family relationships have similarities and differences from other kinds of relationships. Even within families, sin will cause us to label each other and push our expectations and wants onto one another in order that our needs are met. For instance, parents pushing their expectations onto their kids. Children assuming parents provide their needs without personal responsibility or effort and so on. The role you played in your family of origin (the family system in which you were raised) can play an important part in how you relate to other people as an adult. Your family role can define who you are, how you relate to people and how they relate to you and how you see yourself. The role imposed on you, or the one you took on, is very important to understand because it is the role that influences every future relationship in your life. It is crucial to ask yourself, "What role did I play in my family?" and "Who put me into that role?" In examining these questions, it gives clues to type of environment you grew up in and the kinds of relationships you had as a kid.

People who are able to identify the role they played in their family have a powerful tool for changing their lives and improving their present relationships. As mentioned before, these roles are either unconsciously given or the child assumed and maintained the role in order to maintain stability in the family system.

Some of these family and relational roles are:

- **Caretaker**
- **Golden child**
- **Lost Child**
- **Scapegoat or "Problem Child"**
- **Mascot**
- **Hero**
- **The Victim**
- **Rescuer**
- **Persecutor**

You will often see children adopting various roles to help the family function as a stable predictable system. The roles we find ourselves in can be either consistent and stable or fluctuating and spontaneous. For instance, a family members' role can change depending on the current relationship or a certain circumstance encountered at that time. These roles, if not understood, can cause serious relationship problems later on in life.

I counseled a young lady who is the caretaker of her family. At eleven years old, she was a surrogate mother to her five and seven-year-old brothers. She cooked dinner, bathed them, and played mediator, confidant, and counselor to her parents when they fought. She would be there emotionally and physically for everyone else. She stated for many years after, that her brothers considered her their mom. Can you identify with the role she played in her family? Can you relate to her situation?

By understanding the roles we played as kids and still play as adults today, we begin to see the family system and the roles others played within that system. In seeing our past roles, we can see if we are still engaged in those same roles with the same people under similar situations.

By reflecting on our families, we learn what needs we gain by playing those roles. Yes, as odd as it seems we gain something by playing these roles. In **the victim** role, for instance, we gain the attention that was denied to us as children, but what we so desperately crave from others today; in playing **the persecutor,** our need is to have control over others, trying to capture the control others had over us long ago; or by playing **the rescuer,** we will in some way get the importance and value that eluded us by "unconditionally" helping others.

There is a method to our madness in our role-playing, so, what is your "madness"? (See Appendix D for detailed definitions on roles we play.)

As adults, we can no longer view our childhood years and relationships through "rose colored glasses." We must move in the direction of genuine reality and maturity in seeing how our families truly were, identify the sinful behaviors involved, and the present impact our upbringing has on us today.

Earlier in the book, we touched on coping strategies. Many of these strategies are learned from our family of origin. It is important to understand the ways that you learned to cope as a child. Are you still coping in the same way today? Are the coping strategies you use the same as your parents? How do your brothers and sisters cope? We will also discuss ways in which we cope and how coping aids in our survival and in our demise.

There are two overall ways that we cope with stress: **Active and passive** coping strategies are actions that are initiated in order to manage external and or internal stressors that are too demanding for the person to handle. Active coping strategies tend to be more problem focused, or externally focused, in reducing the person's stress. Passive coping strategies are strategies that tend to be more emotion focused or internally, focused to reduce the person's stress.

Active Strategies Include:

- *Confrontational Coping* is the use of aggressive behaviors or other actions to alter the stressful situation (i.e. being verbally or physically controlling toward others to minimize your stress).

- *Seeking Social Support* are actions to gain information, financial, emotional and other forms of help. (i.e. like buying and reading this book or seeking out counseling).

- *Plan Problem Solving* is an intentional focus on solving the problem to alter the situation or to solve it from an analytical perspective (i.e. an alcoholic planning a strategy to avoid hanging out with alcohol and drug using friends).

- *Positive Reappraisal* is the effort to find positive meaning in stressful situations to develop personal growth (i.e. to look at our past and to gain insight and positively reframe what we're learning from it and how it has made us better. What is God teaching us about us through this situation?).

Passive Strategies Include:

- *Distancing* is an effort to detach or to minimize a stressful situation. (i.e. "I don't need to take the trash out tonight, I'll get up early enough"— procrastinating until the last minute then jumping out of bed when we hear the trash truck. I know this coping strategy well!).

- *Self-Controlling* is regulating one's emotions and behaviors (i.e. recognizing yourself feeling overwhelmed and stepping away from the stressful situation to gain emotional balance in order to address the situation appropriately).

- *Accepting Responsibility* is the acknowledgment of one's role in the problem and attempts to correct it (i.e. knowing what your responsible for and not responsible for are crucial elements in problem solving).

- *Escape/Avoidance* is the denial of, wishful or fantasy thinking, or other actions to avoid or not dealing with a problem. This is more of a psychological distancing, not a geographical separation (i.e. believing that you are a failure and fearing that you will disappoint others will likely cause you to procrastinate or not even make an effort to reach your goals).

As children, we were totally dependent on our caregivers for everything. During our childhood years, we developed these strategies of coping in order to survive our childhood environments. We also developed an attachment safeguard called *fantasy bond* with our parents or significant caregivers. This attachment safeguard was developed as a survival mechanism to ensure the child's survival by staying with the parent at all costs. In the book, *The Fantasy Bond: Structure of Psychological Defenses*, Firestone defines a fantasy bond as: "An illusion of connectedness we create with our major caretaker whenever our emotional needs are not adequately met. The fantasy bond is like a mirage in the desert that enables one to survive."[1]

God instilled this connection with our caregivers as a mechanism to keep the dependent child close to the parent— regardless of the parents' behaviors, attitudes or beliefs. God's design was, as long as the child is close to the protection of the parent, it will be okay. This, unfortunately, has not always been the case.

We have seen tragic incidents of parents not only failing to protect their children, but have killed those children God placed in their care. Children are very resilient and can adapt to the harshest of situations by means of certain psychological protective mechanisms. For instance, children who have been severely abused, neglected or victimized have develop amnesia, it is theorized that amnesia kicks in if the fantasy bond is not enough to block out the abusive memories or experiences.

This amnesia occurs to maintain the attachment to the parents. According to noted psychologist and trauma/memory expert, Dr. Freyd:

> Betrayal trauma theory suggests that psychogenic amnesia is an adaptive response in childhood. When a parent or other powerful figure violates a fundamental ethic boundary of human relationships,

---

[1] Robert Firestone, *The Fantasy Bond: Structure of Psychological Defenses* (Santa Barbara: Glendon Association, 1987).

victims may need to remain unaware of the trauma not to reduce suffering but rather to promote survival. Amnesia enables the child to maintain an attachment with a figure vital to survival, development, and thriving.[2]

Another method children use to maintain attachment on behalf of the caregiver is self-blaming. In John Bradshaw's book *Bradshaw On: The Family* he states,

> When parents are abusive and hurt the child…the child will assume the blame, making himself bad…this will maintain the idealized parent belief, so the child feels protected…The more emotionally deprived a person has been, the stronger his fantasy bond…to idealize parents means to idealize the way they raised you (even if it is the parents themselves who are the terror or source of hurt.)[3]

In order for the process of restoration to occur, we must examine our family of origin from a current adult perspective and not from a childish idealized, superficial viewpoint. We must remember, as children we were dependent and vulnerable to our parents or caregivers. As painful as it is, by realistically examining our past family relationships, the pain and hurt that came with it, we begin to integrate our past into our present state of maturity, insightfulness and understanding that brings about closure and peace like the below story demonstrates.

---

[2] Jennifer Freyd, "Betrayal Trauma: Traumatic Amnesia as an Adaptive Response to Childhood Abuse." *Ethics & Behavior* 4 (4) 1994. 307-329.
[3] John Bradshaw, *Bradshaw On: The Family: A New Way of Creating Solid Self Esteem* (Deerfield Beach, FL: HCI 1990).

John's Story

"John" came to counseling struggling with passiveness, co-dependency, low esteem and alcohol abuse. I asked John about his parents and childhood. John initially told me wondrous stories of his relationship with his father and all of the trips and camping they had done together. John was equally as praising to his mother who by all accounts, was an example of what all mothers should be. Upon hearing him describe his parents with such applause and acclaim, an old saying came to mind: "If it sounds too good to be true, then it usually is." John idealized his parental relationship; even though John was well into adulthood, he still held onto a childish sense of security in order to stay attached to them for survival.

I asked John more about his childhood, siblings and his parent's relationships with his siblings. It was not long before John began recognizing inconsistencies in his stories, experiencing painful feelings, and remembering abusive events. John recalled when he was eight years old, his father hitting him so hard, he had to stop because he feared he would leave lasting marks and would be questioned about it by others.

He remembered telling his mother about the incident, and how she made excuses for his fathers' excessive physical abuse. He remembered his mother saying, "Do you want your father to get into trouble?" and "You know your father works hard…you should not have upset him like that."

John began experiencing a multitude of emotions when reflecting back on his childhood. He coped with the feelings and the reality of abuse he endured by having an idealized view of his parents in order to maintain the attachment. Eventually, John used alcohol to numb his feelings of inadequacy and to avoid the fear of being seen as "weak" and the anxiety of being discovered by others.

By self-reflection, self-awareness and self-examination, John was able to see how his relationship with his parents really was and the dysfunctional parenting style in a realistic and mature way. His fantasy bond allowed him to cope with and endure the abusive environment as a helpless dependent child. John was able to see how this childhood abuse negatively impacted his current relationships and view of himself. This enabled him to break the grip of his negative core beliefs about himself, dysfunctional behaviors and relationships.

In challenging his past beliefs, hurts and relationships, it eliminated the immature and insecurities that kept him stuck in a perpetual state of infantilism (immature beliefs, behaviors and thinking). John is now able to continue along the process of healing by experiencing, identifying and expressing emotions without fear of parental retribution. He eventually was able to make the decision to forgive his parents and himself for past actions that brought him pain.

When we begin to acknowledge our parents as less-than-perfect human beings with just as many shortcomings as we have, *we can love and honor them, while not condoning their past decisions or behaviors.* We then are able to move on a path of forgiveness and genuine love on an adult level; not remain stuck in the past by childish fears that hold us hostage in the present.

As children, we were helpless to people, situations, and our environment at that time. Children are incapable of setting boundaries or challenging the choices their parents make. As children, we are at their mercy and rely on them for our every need (physical, emotional, spiritual, etc.). The truth is that some people should not be parents because of the childhood hurts and abuse they experienced. These parents are incapable of investing, uplifting, and pouring themselves into their children's lives. Instead, they tend to be takers, seeing to it that their children meet their needs, instead of meeting their children's needs, as healthy parents should do. These environments and relationships are the catalysts for the very way we see ourselves. Our self-concept has been greatly influenced by how our family felt about and treated us as children.

When children experience encouragement, love, understanding and validation, they believe and see themselves as accepted or "good enough." If children are exposed to violence, abuses, instability and rejection, they are forced into dysfunctional behaviors that become more damaging to them and to the family as a whole. When children are forced into this survival mode, they abandon forethought or the ability to look ahead and see how their behaviors will cause consequences. This emotional stunting is due to the heightened anxiety and vigilance, which inhibits broad progressive thinking. Instead, their focus is exclusively on coping with the present circumstances; surviving the present by any means possible.

If the child is kept in this survival or reactive way of existing, then emotionally he or she remains as a child, but is physically an adult. **Remember**, *an adult who is a child emotionally, is still a child!* They cannot and will not handle adult responsibilities, relationships, or situations appropriately. These individuals have a tendency to be dependent on others. They also tend to avoid or sabotage situations that call for being responsible, mature decision-makers, respect for authority, and being assertive.

Todd's Story

"Todd" was a young man in his late twenties who was unable to keep a job for longer than three months. Todd's employment would often end by him simply not showing up to work without notice or he would be fired for "incompetence."

Todd would often have to be threatened by his parents before he would even look for a job. Todd has lived with his parents most of his life and struggles with drug abuse. When Todd's parents would place household responsibilities on him, in a fit of anger, he would yell and shout at them. On occasion, he would move out and live with friends for a period of time until his friends started demanding he pay his share of expenses. Eventually, Todd would beg his parents to take him back because living on his own is "tough." His parents felt guilt or pity, so they would let him come back home. The cycle started all over again. Our society is raising a generation of "boomerang children"—young adults who are ill equipped to handle adult responsibilities or have mature relationships.

In Paul Hegstorm's book, *Broken Children, Grown-Up Pain*, he outlines present coping behaviors that are exhibited by individuals (like Todd) as a result of early childhood trauma[4]:

- Blocks love and intimacy
- Displays emotional extremes
- Allows no emotions
- Feels suicidal and hopeless
- Is manipulative
- Exhibits no self-control
- Denies problems
- Angry and jealous
- Has a hostile sense of humor

- Has no boundaries
- Considers life as only an existence
- Must prove self
- Is isolated/irritable
- Constantly complains
- Performance-oriented
- Is lonely and distrustful
- Defensive/provoking

[4] Paul Hegstorm, *Broken Children, Grown-Up Pain: Understanding the Effects of Your Wounded Past* (Kansas City: Beacon Hill Press, 2006).

Having an unrealistic view of our past or denial of its effects, only spawns or perpetuates dysfunctional core beliefs and inaccurate memories about ourselves, and others we were in relationships with. We will reconstruct old memories (self-deception) to fit our present beliefs, situations, or relationships, in order to make sense of them or to avoid the pain of remembering them for what they were. In Daniel Schacter's book, *The Seven Sins of Memory: How the Mind Forgets and Remembers* he states,

> Although most of the general public and even many psychologists view memory as something that is fixed in the brain (like a computer file), research has shown that memory is continuously being reconstructed...Old memories are updated with new perceptions, and prior memory traces are replaced. This process occurs outside of consciousness, and the individual does not perceive the new memory as new...The "old" memories that we so confidently treasure may, instead, be the recent suggestions of another person.[5]

For instance, a former client "Mike," had a father who worked a lot and struggled with expressing affection. This type of parental relationship can generate either a real or a perceived core belief in the child's mind (see Appendix D for list of Core Beliefs) that "I am not important or worthy enough." In Mike's case, this core belief was left unchallenged. Over the years, it took on a life of its own, these beliefs were unconsciously expressed by his negative statements about himself. Mike was also an underachiever due to his lack of confidence and poor self-esteem. Eventually these beliefs

---

[5] Daniel Schacter, *The Seven Sins of Memory.*

would manifest into acting out behaviors, such as: substance abuse, anger outbursts, immature acts, etc.

As an adult, Mike continued to pretend his relationship with his father was better than it actually was. *In essence, Mike is presently attempting to recreate a past relationship with his father that never was and will likely never be.* This inner conflict (childhood need vs. present reality) generally leads to various mental health issues and dysfunctional behaviors.

Tools to Use

- Journal painful events from childhood to the present involving mother, father or other significant caregiver.
- Suggested readings:
  On the Family, by John Bradshaw
  Broken Children, Grown-Up Pain, by Paul Hegstorm
  Changing Course, by Claudia Black, Ph.D.

Key Point

Self-reflection is necessary to identify and understand various root causes and core beliefs that emanate from our family of origin. The beliefs that are expressed by present behaviors, attitudes, and thoughts are clues to deep-rooted problems. Self-reflection and awareness can lead to the elimination of assumptions and harmful core beliefs that feed our unconscious drives. These drives manifest into the visible problems present today.

As an adult, the reality is that just because they are your parent(s) does not mean they were or are capable of supplying you with your needs. They are just as hurt, flawed and imperfect as you are. The key is to come to terms with how they have hurt you and how you have taken on more or less responsibility for the relationship. It is crucial to remember that a relationship is a two way street. This rule applies to our parents as well.

Questions to Ponder

1. What are your thoughts and feelings when you think about dad and mom?
2. What unresolved hurts, situations or event(s) that occurred in your family do you refuse to talk about?
3. By not talking about it, who are you protecting? Are you excusing your actions or theirs?
4. How were you mistreated, abused, or neglected by your family, peers, etc.?
5. Which of the above coping behaviors (listed by Hegstrom) do you use?
6. What negative beliefs about yourself have you identified?
7. What is an enemy strategy you've identified that contributes to your hurt and pain?

4

Smoke and Mirrors

"Their malice may be concealed by deception, but their
wickedness will be exposed in the assembly."

– Proverbs 26:26

"The sure way to be cheated is to think one's self more
cunning than others."

– Francois de La Rochefoucauld, French writer
(1613-1680)

I n this chapter, we will discuss the role deception has in
prolonging our suffering and even increasing our
problematic issues. We are going to look at various kinds
of lies and breakdown the cycle of deception, which has
been around since the beginning of time. Eve experienced
being lied to and manipulated by the serpent in the Garden
of Eden. It was the serpent that took some of the truth and
twisted it to get Eve to disobey God by eating of the tree of
the knowledge of good and evil. It was Adam, when
confronted by God, who stated, "It was the woman that you
gave me (blame-shifting) that made me eat of the fruit."
Since the dawn of sin, we have been entangled in it and have
entangled others with it.

Deception, secrets, and lies by their very nature fuel our separation from God and from one another. Deception exists from the very subtle (omission of facts) to the overt (obvious lies & hurtful secrets). Deception toward self and others is the fundamental ingredient and common denominator to many of the hurts, betrayals, and overall dysfunctions that mental health professionals see on a daily basis.

Initially, some clients attempt to deceive the very people who are trying to help them (counselors, family, pastors, etc.). This is done in order to keep their ills, hurts and self-deception from view and their true motives hidden. It is important to understand how deception plays a role in how we see or not see our true selves.

Deception keeps us from seeing (what we perceive) as the painful reality of a given situation. Deception follows fear, hesitancy or apprehension of what is to come (keeping us stagnate and powerless). Deception and fear are intertwined and this union inhibits us from knowing who we really are, because of the fear of what we might see in ourselves or how we might be seen by others. Deception also plays a role in how we see others and how we impact others by our selfish and or destructive action. Let's look at what deception is, what it is not and its variety of forms and degrees.

When someone enters counseling, the first objective in their recovery is for the person to identify and reduce self-deceptive thinking, as well as their need to deceive others through manipulative thoughts and actions that perpetuate destructive behaviors. This deceptive thinking and its resulting dysfunctional behaviors only confirm and strengthen negative core beliefs. Denial is a common form of deception (some of you readers may be in denial as to the severity or extent of your present problem). *Denial* is an unconscious psychological defense mechanism designed to minimize unacceptably painful realities and truths. *Deception* is the act of propagating ideas, beliefs, opinions, and feelings that are false or inundated with half-truths in order for 1) the speaker to misrepresent themselves 2) the speaker manipulates the listener to take an action that benefits the speaker. An example of the insidious use of mass deception comes from Joseph Goebbels, Adolf Hitler's minister of propaganda in order to get the German people to buy into Hitler's vision of a "New Germany." He stated, "If you tell a big enough lie, and keep repeating it, people will eventually come to believe it."

Deception can be used on an individual level (person to person) or on a larger scale like the above example. Other examples are: Jim Jones' Peoples Temple cult, in the 1970s, over 900 of his followers sold all of their possessions and in the end committed suicide; Branch Davidian cult in Waco, Texas when some twenty families shot it out with ATF agents and eventually died when their compound caught fire.

Deception is regularly used to push a multitude of political, products, religious and other social ideologies and agendas on unsuspecting groups or populations. Deception more commonly occurs on an individual level. For instance, a driver is pulled over for speeding and tells the police officer he was just informed a relative is in serious condition in the hospital. The police officer gives the driver a warning and lets him go. The driver has lied about having a relative in the hospital in order to avoid the consequences of a getting a speeding ticket.

Deception clouds our view of reality and of ourselves. When we deceive others, we are in turn, deceiving ourselves with equal strength and delusion. In Charles Ford's book,

Lies, Lies, Lies: The Psychology of Deceit, he describes three levels of lying.[6]

- **The first level** is lying to manipulate the behaviors of others, without trying to influence their beliefs (as referenced in the above example of the driver).

- **The second level** is when the liar is aware of the listener's beliefs and aware of the fact that their lie may change those beliefs. For example; a drug-abusing son lies to his mother about the severity of his drug use by saying, "I have it under control. Don't worry about it mom."

- **The third level** involves the liar's need to be believed by the listener. The liar sees value in the listener's acceptance of the lie; the liar is self-deceived into thinking that the lie he told has good or truthful intentions behind it.

God exposes, and unveils the methods Satan uses to trap us and God provides ways to detect, avoid, or escape them.

Satan has a plan to keep us stuck, failing to live life more abundantly. When we are stuck, we become more and more desperate to be saved, eventually we will either get tired and give up or reach for anything that will rescue us from this temporary hell were in. This is where Satan comes along and presents what looks like a life preserver to a drowning person, but in reality, it is a rope with a noose attached to an anvil.

Satan and his demonic forces want to deceive us and move us away from dependence on God. Satan desires that we trust in our own frail, inconsistent, and narrow-minded

---

[6] Charles V. Ford, *Lies! Lies! Lies! The Psychology of Defeat*, (Arlington, VA: American Psychiatric Publishing, 1999).

ways. He counts on us to reach for the quick fix or the easy way out. More importantly, he depends on us not to ask the Lord for guidance, wisdom and patience regarding our current situation.

The entire world system gravitates toward three extreme ideologies:

1. That tangible things of this world will bring happiness and security.

2. That people are the "Masters of their destiny" (demi-gods) and are in complete control.

3. That instant gratification is preferred over delayed rewards and being patient is not necessary.

Satan deceives us into believing we have control, which is the epitome of self-deceptive thinking, and is what the serpent in the Garden used to deceive Eve into eating the apple. In Genesis 3:4-5, the serpent said to the woman. "For God knows that when you eat of it your eyes will be opened, and you will be like God, knowing good and evil." The fact is, we can't even control what will happen in the next five minutes, let alone, to foolishly attempt to control others and our futures! It is important to plan, but we are fooling ourselves in thinking we have control of that future.

Our sinful nature tends to exacerbate the relentless pursuit of control, fleshly pleasures, power, prestige, money, possessions, and leisure. Seeking the approval of others has proven time and time again to derail us from God's purpose for our lives. Some of these things are not wrong in themselves, but when our strong desire for them overshadows God's intent for us having them, this can turn even good things into idols.

As mentioned above, there are many examples of man's sinful nature taking the Word of God and twisting it in order to deceive and to justify and rationalize sinful behaviors and defiling His glorious creations (sex and marriage being the targets of sinfulness). In order to recognize the enemy's use of deception in our lives, we must also recognize the ways our community is vulnerable to the enemy's schemes and how the world is being enslaved by those schemes.

It is important to remember that the deceptive schemes of the enemy are not always evident as a giant wave—they can come in the form of harmless ripples or as morning dew. Often, the very thing that entices us deceives us: a pretty face, opportunities to make money, a shot at fame, a momentary escape from discomfort, or doing what is "acceptable" to others, etc. The temptation appears harmless enough at first, but like all schemes of the enemy, there is a price to pay for participating.

Joanne's Story

Joanne, a bright twenty-three year-old college student was eager to be in a relationship with Matt, a young man she met on campus. Matt was bright and charismatic, everything Joanne always wanted in a man. However, what Joanne did not know was that Matt struggled with prescription drugs and alcohol abuse. Joanne told her family and friends all about her new love interest. Matt was very secretive about his use around her and her family. Over time, Joanne became vested in the relationship. She started to suspect Matt's drug use, but did not want to confront him (believing she would lose him in the process—*self-deceptive thinking (denial) taking form.* She was afraid she would be alone.

Matt introduced Joanne to marijuana, "I think you just need to relax baby," said Matt. He was *deceiving Joanne in order to deceive himself into continued use,* Matt felt guilty about his use.

He manipulated Joanne into using drugs in order to avoid the guilty feelings of using drugs alone, which is second-level lying. Joanne felt she needed to be loved and accepted, and she would do anything to have it.

In this case, Joanne idolized her relationship with Matt instead of prioritizing her relationship with God. This fit into Matt's desire to avoid feelings of guilt and being judged about his use. As time went on, Joanne's use increased and her behavior coincided with Matt's drug lifestyle.

Joanne's friends began to notice a significant difference in her demeanor and attitude. Her grades dropped and her drinking increased as well. Joanne's friends confronted her, but Joanne did not see her use as a problem (denial). As for Matt, he could do no wrong as far as Joanne was concerned. According to Joanne, "He'll stop using when he gets that job he has recently applied for…" That job is bartending at a local pub where Matt has sold and purchased drugs in the past.

Joanne has been deceived by Matt, and has deceived herself in order to maintain the fantasy of her relationship. Maintaining this fantasy fosters Joanne's denial of the realities and the effects of their drug and alcohol abuse on others and themselves. According to Ford, "Lies are used to bridge the gap between fantasy, expectations, or assumptions with reality."[7]

Intent is an important component of deception. For deception to occur, the intent to misdirect others is required. In an honest mistake however, there is no intent to deceive or misdirect the listener/receiver. You have already learned about the three levels of lying. Let's look at the forms of lies commonly used:

---

[7] Charles Ford, *Lies! Lies! Lies! The Psychology of Defeat,* 130.

1. **Relationship lies**: Social lies that are used to "break the ice" for smoother interpersonal interaction. Example: Someone who says, "I love your new hair style," even though the opposite is true.

2. **Comedic lies**: Lies told strictly to poke fun and to entertain the listener (exaggeration is a key part of this lie).

3. **Protective lies**: Lies told to ease suffering or increase self-esteem. Example: During World War II, the Dutch told the Nazis they had not seen any Jewish people, when in fact, the Dutch resistance were hiding Jewish people to protect them.

4. **Defensive lies**: Lies told to protect oneself or to avoid punishment (children will lie to implicate other children for something they have done to avoid punishment).

5. **Angry lies**: Lies told to inflict harm on someone, or to gain some leverage in a situation (girls who are jealous of other girls may spread lies in order to vent or project their own shortcomings and anger onto others).

6. **Pathological lies**: These are lies told for little or no reason. This may be done unconsciously to gain attention, acceptance, or to escape current realities.

7. **Pseudologia Fantastica**: Lies that are initially believable, but the liar continues to fabricate the stories, creating inconsistencies (i.e. criminals may start out mixing truths and lies, but the more they tell their stories, the more inconsistencies and the more unbelievable their alibis become).

Tools to Use

1. Spend quality time in the Word and prayer; reflecting on honesty and how you are meeting your relational needs.
2. Approach five close and trusted people in your life; ask them the following:
    a) "How am I as a friend, brother, sister, etc to you?
    b) "How do I deceive, manipulate or lie to others?
    c) "How do I deceive myself?

Key Point

As we continue on our journey of self-discovery and understanding, we have discussed various types of deception and lies the enemy has and continues to use in an effort to blind us to God's truth about our uniqueness and strengths, as well as our weaknesses and pain. We have learned how deception comes at us, either from a friend, a beautiful woman or handsome man, through fame, money or the implied promise of desires.

Deception, whether from others or self-generated, is:

1. Our pitiful way of negating the reality of our moral existence.
2. Our attempt at avoiding our finiteness, our lack of control and limitations.
3. The vain effort to numb the pain and hurt within ourselves.
4. Rationalizing the need to avoid confronting those responsible for our hurt, shame and discontent.

It is our deception that continues the behaviors we become so reliant on, and it is deception that stays in the shadows and will fight not to be exposed.

Deception is a psychological buffer that is helpful in allowing us to view the world without being overwhelmed by the harshness and intensity of reality; however, deception can be overused, blinding us to the extent of our problematic behaviors and to its harmful impact on others. Deception prohibits us from seeing the truth of our condition so we are able to address it appropriately. *Being dependent on deception in order to cope with the everyday stressors of life is, by far, one of the most debilitating struggles we will face when it comes to healing.*

Questions to Ponder

1. How are you rationalizing your current negative behaviors, thoughts and feelings?
2. Are you currently excusing someone else's actions that hurt you?
3. What is keeping you from seeking help for your problem(s)?
4. What are you in denial about at this very moment?
5. What type of lies do you tell most often? Whom do you tell them to?
6. Have you been abused by a family member? If so, how are you deceiving yourself or others about it?
7. How do members of your family manipulate, lie, or deceive others in or outside your family?

5

Moths to the Flame

"We feel free when we escape-even if it be but from the
frying pan to the fire."

— Eric Hoffer

"No temptation has overtaken you except what is common
to mankind. And God is faithful; He will not let you be
tempted beyond what you can bear. But when you are
tempted, He will also provide a way out so that you can
endure it."

— 1 Corinthians 10:13

In this chapter, we will discuss the role that desires and
temptations play in our dysfunctions, and what the Word
says about them and how to address them. We will also
examine how desires manifest into behaviors (behaviors are
our means to meet those desires and needs) and the
consequences that are the result.

In life, we are and will always be tempted by the desires,
pleasures, and wants of this world. We are consistently being
bombarded, saturated and pressured by images, ideas, and
other social expectations that are set all around us that appeal
to the immediate satisfaction of the flesh.

The desires and temptations of this world are alluring and can be difficult to resist. I like using the analogy of a trap with bait and how it to draws the prey. For instance, a monkey will reach its hand into a trap to grab an irresistible piece of fruit or a shining object. The monkey's hand is stuck because it will not let go to the bait. It is the greed of the monkey that provides its own captivity. The monkey is unaware that it simply has to let go to be free.

When we have desires and temptations, they in themselves are not sinful. However, when we prioritize the desire to achieve goals that reach our temptations to satisfy—over God, family, or relationships—we are eventually lead into behaviors that are harmful and inappropriate. We have now sinned.

The Word of God states, "The wage of sin is death." By entertaining desires and temptations, we start creating blueprints for sin's construction and our eventual destruction. A major characteristic of unhealthy desires and temptation is secrecy. Our desires and temptations are birthed and evolve in the darkness of shame, jealousy, and desperation, as well as other painful feelings and negative core beliefs. As our desire and temptation matures, it is shown to all as sin. We eventually succumb to temptations, desires, and wants without regard for others. Our only desire is to meet our desires and needs, nothing else matters. We also underestimate the control sin has in our life. We will do whatever it takes to achieve it, we will even convince others of the necessity for the desire as well as rationalize the behaviors in order to meet our neediness and conceal our hurt.

When we encounter life's struggle with sin, we must first understand two important aspects of what our struggle is with sin. First, let's define what a struggle is. *A struggle is being in contention with an adversary or opposing force.* The struggle comes from dispelling, challenging or changing the influence temptation and desires have on us. The three important aspects of understanding our struggle with desires and/or our temptations are:

1. What are the underlying desires or temptations we wish to fulfill?
2. What are we sacrificing in order to meet our desires?
3. Why is it important for us to meet these desires?

It is just as important to understand what drives our sinful behaviors, as well as knowing our sinful behaviors themselves. As mentioned before, we also struggle with ambivalence. *Ambivalence is having two opposite ideas or beliefs about the same issue.* It is ambivalence that often causes inner conflict when we engage in sinful behaviors or behaving in a manner that is counter to what we know or believe to be right or wrong. For instance, when we casually view pornography, romanticize or recreationally use drugs, or compromise our values for money or notoriety, we now move from being tempted to embracing and entertaining our desires. The results are:

1. We temporarily "feel good," but are in a state of "tunnel vision" ignoring future consequences of our actions.

2. We add onto our existing shame and pain by the consequences of our current dysfunctional actions.

3. We continue the cycle. When we give in to our desires, they will ultimately keep us stagnate emotionally and stuck in our current problematic cycle.

The Apostle Paul knew all too well this duality of the mind and spirit and the pain it causes.

> "I do not understand what I do. For what I want to do I do not do, but what I hate I do."
>
> – Romans 7:15

Struggles are often synonymous with situations, relationships, or events that go with or against our values, assumptions, expectations, and wants of life. Depending on how you view your struggles, they can be opportunities to understand your shortcomings, issues, and hurts. The Word is very clear on how we should view struggles, desires and the setbacks in life. Let's examine what God says about our struggles and ways to overcome them:

> "Consider it pure joy, my brothers, whenever you face trials of many kinds, because you know that the testing of your faith develops perseverance. Perseverance must finish its work so that you may be mature and complete, not lacking anything."
>
> – James 1:2-4

The struggle itself, is only the foreground of a more pervasive threat—our fleshly desires for acceptance and the temptation in gaining value in ourselves by making others, our financial, occupational or religious status more important than God. In entertaining these desires, we only serve to increase our desire for more. These hedonistic pleasures might even get to a point where we deceive ourselves into believing we are entitled to them, or that it is our right to possess what we want.

God has given us the ability to adapt to our surroundings, adaptation is a way we survive abrupt changes and adverse conditions life throws at us. Adaptation has allowed human beings to survive and thrive as a species. Adaptation is not only an ability to deal with change, but it allows us to become accustom to it, regardless what it is. However, Adaptation has a flip side or destructive aspect. As we continue to desire more and more, we adapt to our present desire level. The destructive aspect of adaptation to our desires is the increase tolerance to unhealthy behaviors, beliefs and attitudes. In the case of pornography, the increasing danger is in the level of deviance or graphic nature of the material, and the frequency of viewing, which increases in order to receive the same level of arousal. In substance abuse, the danger is in the increasing amount used, drug potency and frequency of use to gain the same "high" as the first time. This behavior is what leads to riskier behaviors.

We also enter a cycle of increased use of denial and deception to rationalize our appetite for the desires we want. Our increased need to achieve these desires will in turn, perpetuate our use of self-deception, which rationalizes our action thus leading to continual dependency on sinful behaviors to meet those initial desires. By acting sinfully to meet our desires and needs, we hurt others and ourselves along the way. In the process, we produce greater shame and regret, only to continue the cycle all over again.

It is crucial to see an accurate view of what our desires are, how we pursue them and how they lead to internal and external consequences. Only then can we stop the insidious cycle of temptation, desires, disastrous behaviors and the consequences they have on others and ourselves. The exercise below can help to accurately show the consequences of our behaviors as well as, help us reflect on the "reality" of present and future consequences of action or not taking action will have.

I developed the **Consequential Effect Continuum** (CEC) to assists the individual in reflecting on present destructive behaviors, thoughts and feelings and in breaking down the immediate or potential consequences by time (present and future) and it's relational locations; i.e. internal effects: inner emotional, spiritual and psychological effects, impressions or beliefs and/or external effects: it's effects on relationship with others and life circumstances.

Present/Internal: These are **present thoughts, feelings, perceptions and beliefs** we experience due to an outer experience encountered.

Present/External: This is our present exterior self that others can see, such as: behaviors, attitudes, moods or circumstances that are creating the most problems (i.e. drug abuse, martial affairs, porn addictions and so on).

Future/Internal: These are potential thoughts, feelings, emotions and beliefs that are likely to occur in the future, if the Present/External situation is left unchanged.

Future/External: Understanding how behaviors, attitudes, moods circumstances and situations will manifest themselves in the future. For instance, present uncontrolled drinking will eventually lead to future health problems, jail, etc.

Below is an example of CEC:

Present circumstance: I was arrested for DUI

Present

Internal: Right now, I feel guilty, embarrassed, and ashamed for going to jail.

External: The legal cost, attorney fees, loss of driving privileges, fearful of how friends and family will feel and treat me from now on.

Future

> **Internal**: I will likely feel regret, anger and disappointment about the arrest and decision to drink and drive.

> **External**: My arrest will negatively affect any future job opportunities or advancement; will cause mistrust with others.

The **Reward Effect Continuum** (REC) is similar to CEC, but assists individuals in **reflecting on the positive effects of stopping harmful behaviors, thoughts, or feelings.** REC uses the above scale such as time, intensity of positive effect of ceased behavior on the individual and the relational location. Let's look at an REC example.

Present Circumstance: I am no longer drinking alcohol

Present

> **Internal**: I feel proud of myself for seeing the problem before it got worse.

> **External**: By not drinking, I avoid the possibility of being arrested, fines, and/or hurting others.

Future

Internal: I will be more self-confident in the decisions I make and the way I feel about myself.

External: I will not put myself in a situation where I will risk my life or the lives of others, or cause more financial, relational problems with family and friends.

𝒥ools to 𝒰se

1. Journaling encounters with daily temptations and desires. Examine how the "enemy" is using these worldly trappings to keep you stagnate and distant from God.
2. On a separate sheet of paper, utilize the CEC and REC exercise (discussed above).
3. With a close friend, therapist, spouse or family members, discuss your struggles with temptations and desires. Try and pinpoint the locations, times, surrounding circumstances and people that may trigger those desires and the harmful behaviors.

𝒦ey 𝒫oint

It is critical that we realize our persistent lean toward our fleshly weakness to temptation and our willingness to fulfill our desires at any cost. The Word of God empowers us to learn from the experiences of others as well as our own, so we may live the kind of life that helps us realize our potential and how our uniqueness and potentiality glorifies God. The Word reminds us that we are more than the "things" of this world. We are in fact spiritual beings experiencing a mortal existence. The Word of God is our "spiritual guardrail" that keeps us away from the beautiful, but deadly, hypnotic glow of sin's flame.

Questions to Ponder

1. What temptations/desires do you struggle with?

2. What do you gain/lose from meeting your desires?

3. How are you going to address your temptations and desires from now on?

4. How have you seen God's role in your struggles: punishing, judgmental, absent, as a puppeteer, loving, etc.?

5. After doing the CEC and REC exercises, has your **view** of your current struggle(s) changed? How has the struggle itself changed? Has it stayed the same?

6

When Worlds Collide

"Feelings come and feelings go. There is no need to fear
them and no need to crave them. Let them come, and then
let them go. No feeling is your permanent reality, no matter
how intense it is."

— Anonymous

"Peace is not the absence of conflict, but the ability to cope
with it."

— Anonymous

I n this chapter, we will discuss the world of emotions and
feelings. We will define them as well as examine how they
work and the role they play in our lives. We will also look
at our thinking self and it's characteristics. By understanding
our two worlds and bring them into unison, we are able to
gain inner awareness, identify and express our emotional self
in a way that is appropriate, articulate and accurate so others
may connect with us and we with them. We will first examine
our emotional self and learn how this intimidating and often
misunderstood aspect of ourselves aids us in relationship
development and in our everyday survival.

In his book, *Emotions Revealed* (2003): Paul Ekman, noted psychologist and body language expert, states,

> Emotions can, and often do, begin very quickly, so quickly, in fact, that our conscious self does not participate in or even witness what in our mind triggers an emotion at any particular moment. That speed can save our life in an emergency, but it can also ruin our lives when we overreact…it is possible, though not easy, to make some changes in what triggers our emotions and how we behave when we are emotional…Emotions are reactions to matters that seem to be very important to our welfare… Emotions prepare us to deal with important events without our having to think about what to do. You would not have survived that near-miss car accident if part of you weren't continually monitoring the world for signs of danger. The subconscious reacts to an emotional trigger fear=brake, steer, etc.[8]

Emotions are God given and it is our responsibility to understand and express them in an honest and genuine way. Emotions that are experienced, understood and properly expressed are the most effective healing and relationship developing tool available. God never makes a mistake; it is only when man attempts to avoid, misunderstands and misuses God's gifts for his own self-gratification that brings about our pain and suffering. *Emotions have never killed anyone, it is how we chose to cope with the emotions that kills us.* It is our willingness to experience and express authentic emotions, that allow us to survive in crisis situations and communicate our understanding of them and their impact on our lives. We

---

[8] Paul Ekman, 19–20.

will examine in greater detail what are feelings and emotions, as well as what makes them different and crucial for a healthy life. Understanding this differentiation aids us in experiencing, identifying and expressing emotions appropriately.

What are Feelings?

I believe feelings are physiological sensations we experience when we encounter a particular person, event, or situation. The particular perception or relationship we have with the situation, event or person will not only influence the feelings we will experience, they will also affect the intensity and duration of those feelings as well. For example: Have you ever been called into your boss's office for a private meeting you did not expect to have that day? What type of relationship did you have with your boss prior to the meeting? Was it hostile? Or Friendly? What were you physically feeling before, during, and after the meeting? Perhaps you felt tightness in your stomach, or a rapid heartbeat? By focusing your attention on how a situation, event, or person makes you physically feel and translating that feeling into words, you are able to give it an emotional label. The emotion you label the situation, person, or event tells what value and/or importance it has to you at that time. Feelings move in one direction, forward to completion. Feelings will go through a series of stages:

1. Our feelings are often triggered by a person, a time of day, event, situation, memory, etc.

2. The feeling's intensity will increase, depending on what significance the person places on the surrounding circumstances, relationships, or situation. The feeling could rise slowly or rise quickly in intensity.

3. The feeling will peak at its highest point (the more intense the feeling, the more inhibited our thinking becomes).

4. Over time, the situation changes or resolves itself, thereby reducing the intensity of the emotion.

5. As the emotion drops, our increased thinking initiates self-reflection for what just occurred. This can produce additional emotions such as guilt, regret, etc. (depending on how the situation was handled).

It is crucial to not only define how we feel, but also to understand how our present situations are impacted by our past experiences. These present situations are in some ways similar to a past situation. How we dealt with the past situation will be how we deal with the present one. When the past intrudes upon the present, this causes a physiological reaction, which must be identified and acknowledged. Only by recognizing what is occurring, breaking it down into understandable segments, and talking about what we have learned and experienced with others can we find meaning to and a solution for this dilemma.

What are Emotions?

I believe emotions are the cognitive labels we use to identify the physiological sensations (feelings) brought on by daily encounters with various persons, events, and or situations. For instance, the physiological sensations of rapid and shallow breathing, tightening of the muscles, and a raised voice, are feelings we experience when we are accused of doing something we did not do. We associate or emotionally label these with physical feelings as anger, hostility, or frustration.

Common Characteristics of our Emotional Self Include:

- We experience, but are presently unaware of physiological changes taking place.
- Emotional episodes can be brief (lasting for seconds) or longer. It may move into a mood (lasting for a day or longer).
- It is significant and is perceived as "real" to the person experiencing the emotion.
- Emotions happen to us, they are not chosen by us.
- We become emotional about things that are relevant to our ancestral or cultural heritage.
- The desire to experience or avoid an emotion motivates many of our behaviors.
- Our affect (how well we physically express or show our emotions) informs others of how the person is feeling and the value they place on the triggering situation, person, or event.

God created us to be emotionally needy. We were created this way in order to promote togetherness and intimacy. When we can identify and express our emotional needs such as: *Affection, Appreciation, Approval, Attention, Comfort, Encouragement, Support, Security, Respect, and Acceptance.* We communicate these needs to others in order to get what we need from them and vice versa. By expressing our emotional needs to others, we send the messages that we trust them *and* that they are important to us. Meeting the needs of others and in turn, having our needs met, enhances *well-being* and furthers our survival as a species.

There have been numerous scientific studies and collected evidence that strongly suggest to maintain emotional and physical health, we need emotional affirmation, validation, and physical connection with others. An undisputed fact is that love and intimacy affect health and facilitate recovery from a variety of illness such as Irritable Bowel Syndrome, migraines, and ulcers, just to name a few. In his book, *Love & Survival: The Scientific Basis for the Healing Power of Intimacy*, Dean Ornish, MD writes:

> Love and intimacy are at the root of what makes us sick and what makes us well…I am not aware of any factor in medicine—not diet, not smoking, not stress, not genetics, not drugs, not surgery—that has greater impact on our quality of life…

When we receive "strokes" or praise from others, this is strong motivation for interaction. People seek out all of the above needs through connection; needs are exchanged through strokes. Strokes can be physical or verbal. Physical strokes are any form of touch: hugs, kisses, caresses, backrubs, holding hands, or being held. Verbal strokes are statements that acknowledge some feature of another person in a positive way. Verbal strokes can be about a person's looks, clothing, intelligence, generosity, creativity or any other attribute the person possesses.

Our emotional needs are not only strong influences on our behavior, but they also express what I believe are the current conditions of our relationships. For instance, when we take the time to play with our children, they are receiving the emotional needs of **Attention, Affection** and **Acceptance**. When we avoid our children or manipulate them to do what *we* want to do, they are denied key emotional needs. The lack of these vital needs are interpreted as rejection, inadequacy, or a feeling of being unworthy. Many of our past emotional experiences ***will*** determine aspects of our present relationships, such as: how close, distant, ridged, or chaotic the relationship will be.

Karen Horney, an early twentieth century psychologist said, "There are generally three types of relational approaches: 1) Those who move toward others 2) those who move against others and 3) those who move away from others." We will discuss Karen Horney's approaches in greater detail.

In **type 1, move toward others,** this person is generally a people-pleaser in order to avoid making others upset or cause any uncomfortable feelings around them. The manipulative style of this person is that they are unconsciously more interested in changing others emotions or moods, rather than dealing with their own emotions. They will convince themselves and others they are "good Samaritans" out to bring happiness and contentment to the world, when, in fact, they are selfishly attempting to manipulate the emotions of others around them to make the situation they're in more comfortable or to feel good about themselves.

In **type 2, moving against others**, this person will rebel or push others away in order to avoid getting hurt. They could be in a good relationship with a caring person; however, as the relationship develops and the type 2 person feels more vulnerable, the type 2 will sabotage the relationship by pushing the other away (before they get hurt first). In their minds and hearts, they see close intimate relationships as something they long for and want, but also see it as a major source of pain to avoid.

In **type 3, moving away from others**, this person is the avoider. They avoid connecting with others by physical distance or being emotionally guarded. This person generally avoids social settings and has a strong fear of bringing attention to them. They often use silence or agreeableness (telling others what they want to hear) as a means to stop the direction of the conversation by taking the focus off of them entirely. Their motive is to keep others from seeing their perceived selves (i.e. the inner self they believe others can see). This perceived self is filled with fear, perceived defects, inadequacies and self-doubt.

God created us to be relational, to be connected to one another. As unique creations of God, He has us all connected to each other. This connectedness is what helps us through life's toughest challenges and sustains us by allowing the expression of that precious inner self that conveys trust and love to one another. This connectedness is essential for life. For instance, a plant is connected to the soil for food and to the sun for energy and so on. What if a bucket were to be placed over the plant? Well, it will die from the lack of sunlight. What if the plant were pulled out of the ground? Again, it will die from the lack of food and water in the soil. The opposite is true as well; if a plant had too much water or too much sun then it will die. Like the plant, if we are relationally too enmeshed or dependent on others, it can be emotionally draining and eventually kill the relationship. **We are no different.** As God's wondrous creations, we were meant for balance, harmony and peace. We were also not meant to constantly live on the edge, pushing the envelope or burning both ends of the candle. These ideas are man's need to "feel the rush," "keep up with the Joneses" or to have control. The below exercise assist us in self-reflection and emotional awareness.

Emotions Exercise

In order to gain self-awareness—and later self-understanding—the ability to identify feelings and emotions, as well as express those feelings and emotions is a crucial skill that needs constant practice. First, list twenty-five feelings and or emotions on a sheet of paper. Next to each feeling or emotion, write a brief definition of each one. Write a situation in which you felt that emotion or feeling. If you cannot think of a situation you may make up a situation where that feeling or emotion may be felt. For example:

- ***Ashamed***: Feeling inferior, inadequate, or embarrassed.
- ***Situation:*** I was ashamed of myself for driving while being drunk.

This exercise truly helps the person to integrate the head (thinking) by reflecting on past or present situations, relationships or events that coincided with the emotion. The heart (emotions) experiences the past or present emotions felt and links situation to the emotion. When this integration occurs, the person is now genuine and accurate in the expression of emotion and the situation that triggered it. They are on their way to becoming more open to honest relationships with others, becoming healthier individuals in the process.

Our Thinking Self

For restoration to occur, we must understand both the emotional self, as well as the thinking, reasonable logical self. I believe thinking is the intentional application of sound facts, observation and logic to our daily relationships and circumstances. It is the thinking self that allows us to apply new restorative knowledge, and dispel antiqued dysfunctional beliefs. In the thinking state, we can apply logic and reason to our denial and misperceptions of others, God and ourselves; when we deliberately shift our attention into thinking mode, our emotions begin to subside (The thinking mode increases our ability to make proper choices, even during stressful situations); our thinking self breaks down past and present experiences in order to gain clarification, understanding and to acquire control of our impulses. Our thinking self allows us to see life more objectively; exposing more options and choices to us that otherwise would have been hidden from our view.

It is only when the two worlds are in sync, the head (thinking, reflection, processing, etc.) and the heart (emotions, intimacy with others, expression) are connected and working in unison, that balance, peace, and contentment in and around us is achieved.

Tools to Use

1. Use the above emotional exercise to reflect on your emotional self and to log past and present emotional experiences.
2. Learn and apply the "I feel….About….Because…" format. (See Appendix A).
3. Spend quality time alone (go for a walk, read the Word, etc.) to think about your current life condition and relationships.

Key Point

Every day brings a variety of situations that spark particular feelings, which trigger corresponding thoughts. The interaction between our feelings and thoughts result in behaviors. Our feelings, thoughts, behaviors, and beliefs *has* far more to tell us about who we are, what we value, what we experienced, and who we are not, then we give them credit. The questions we ask are paramount to eliminating ignorance, *becoming* aware, developing personal growth and character.

It is vital to understand how emotions are in fact questions in disguise. For instance, **confusion** = *"why aren't I getting the results I want or expect?"* **depression** = *"No matter how much I try I can't stop these feelings or change my circumstances to the way I want or expect them to be."* and **anxiety** = *"I am worried and afraid I will not get what I should or expect to have."* By examining our life with specific questions, in a particular order, we begin to learn more about why we feel, think and behave in certain ways. We also learn why—under certain circumstances—we have certain emotions and how they drive us to act in particular ways. Only by refusing to be slaves to our emotional selves, but also, not neglecting them either; do we retain the balance we are striving for, an equal partnership of emotion tapered by a measurable dose of logic and reasoning. This brings our two worlds together in unison and harmony. Not only does it add spice to life, but also clarity and understanding as well.

Questions to Ponder

1. Do you move *toward, against* or *away from* others as discussed earlier in this chapter?
2. *Which part do* you struggle with *the most?*
    a. *feeling* emotions
    b. *identifying* feelings or emotions
    c. being able to *express* feelings
3. Are there certain people you move toward, away from, or against?
4. How do you feel right now? What is causing you to feel this way?
5. Are you more of a *thinker, doer* (hands on, always busy) or *feeler?*
6. What are the advantages and disadvantages of the present way you express yourself?

7

Persistence of Pain

"Pain is inevitable. Suffering is optional."

– Anonymous

"In the depths of every heart, there is a tomb and a dungeon, though the lights, the music and revelry above may cause us to forget their existence."

– Nathaniel Hawthorne, *The Haunted Mind*

In this chapter, we will differentiate between pain and suffering. We will explore how both pain and suffering assist in healing and how they can undermine our efforts for recovery. We will look at what God says about addressing our hurt.

Ever since the Garden of Eden, we have become separated from God due to our sin. As human beings, we are consistently bombarded by, exposed to, afflicted, and inundated with the pain caused by the poor choices of others, as well as, the pain we inflict onto ourselves either unintentionally or intentionally.

In our desperate quest to be in control—despite the cost to others and the pain we receive, in many respects—we are trying to be in control of the uncontrollable or god-like. In our indelible lust for supremacy, we have and continue to suffer, not just from the sinful nature we inherited, but also from our unquenchable desire to be all-powerful, expecting no consequences for this choice.

It is interesting, as well as ironic, that the more we submit ourselves to the Will of our Heavenly Father, the less we suffer. Since we are imperfect and fallible, does it make any sense to try to control others and everything else around us?

Think about it: if you had an open handful of sand and slowly started to close it, by the time your hand was fully closed, would you have more or less sand than when it was opened? You would probably find you have far less sand with a closed fist than an open hand. This is so when we attempt to control our world out of fear, insecurities and desperation. Our attempt to control our world is really a cry to the world that we are afraid. Control is an illusion of security for those struggling with insecurities. Control is a fantasy, wrapped in denial, surrounded by fear.

Mortal life is filled with uncertainty and pain. So often, life does not go the way we would like. It does us no good to pretend we can control it, except to understand it and how it affects us and how to appropriately express, and address it. Pain is a condition of our existence. Pain tells us; 1) How we have been hurt 2) The intensity of pain is an indicator of how meaningful the person, situation event is to us. 3) The pain itself can tell us how to address it (if we avoid or numb the pain, we can't address it).

Can we escape death? No, we can't. So, does it make sense that we can escape pain? If you feel no pain then, Amen! You are either with our Heavenly Father in paradise or high as a kite assuming some strange yoga position on your sofa! But neither are happening since you are reading this book.

Types of Pain

It is important to identify and understand what pain is before we can work to resolve it and move on. Pain is, of course, an uncomfortable condition that manifests itself in a number of ways: **physical, emotional, spiritual** or **psychological.** We can experience pain from within (self-inflicted) or from others.

Pain can be unintentionally as well as intentionally caused. For instance, pain that is the result of a natural disaster like an earthquake or hurricane, is traumatic indeed; it causes loss of life, property damage, etc. This is an unintentional outside source of pain we experience. People are more liking to recovery from this type of pain because there is no motive behind it; it is a naturally occurring event that is devoid of intention, and (natural disasters do not personally target the individual).

Now, the pain at the hands of our fellow man—well it's not just the painful action, but what lies behind their terrible action—can be more traumatic, personally taken and heart-wrenching than anything else the victim could experience. For instance, a family is put through a great deal of emotional, spiritual, and financial hardships and pain because a drunk driver kills the father and his eight-year-old daughter.

The victim's surviving family members are left to question the motive of the driver and reasons why he would put others' lives at risk? Had he driven drunk before this? We instinctually want to know, as victims of another's actions, is it a mistake of the mind? Or, is it the action of the heart?

An example of self-inflicted hardship would be, a husband and father who struggles with a debilitating addiction to pornography and alcohol. Instead of being honest about the extent of his addiction, he tries to minimize its grip on him. One evening, while his family is out and after several drinks, he passes out in front of the television, while

81

in the act of masturbating to an erotic video. Upon their return home, his wife and kids seeing him passed out with the video on. He is awakened to the disappointment and disgusted look on their faces. Pain is generally a temporary condition, however, when we chose to ignore it, it festers and becomes chronic in nature. It spreads into other areas of our life like a cancer. It becomes greater than its original cause. We will examine how pain eventually manifests into suffering.

Suffering Defined

Let's examine suffering and its role in recovery. Suffering is defined by the Word as "enduring pain, hardship or loss." When we suffer, as mentioned earlier, it can be at the hands of others or by our own. Suffering is often an unintentional prolonging of pain, hardship and the reluctance to acknowledge or resolve an issue, as well as to accept what we lost. Suffering includes pain, discomfort and hurt, however, pain doesn't necessarily include suffering. In a nutshell, how we deal with or avoid our hurt and issues will determine if we experience pain or continue to suffer indefinitely.

It is important to understand that we have and will experience pain, but we do not have to suffer. In counseling, I often see clients who are in a constant state of suffering. They and many others, suffer because they want control, they want their present circumstances to be something it is not. They procrastinate on what they should do which in turn, perpetuates their suffering. An important question to ask ourselves is: Are we suffering due to a mistake of the mind, or are we suffering due to actions of the heart? In the next section, we will examine this concept and how it relates to healing.

Mind and Heart: A Mistake or Intentional?

Let us define and examine if the pain we are experiencing is a result of a mistake of the mind or actions of the heart? **A mistake of the mind** is when someone made an error in judgment or an incorrect decision with no intention of inflicting harm or pain onto others. For instance, a pilot working a sixteen hour day who must fly another six hours to end his shift, makes a critical flight miscalculation which causes the death of himself and another 123 passengers. Was it his intention to kill himself and all of the passengers? No, of course not, but would his actions be more or less forgivable than, someone who intentionally wanted to cause the death of another, like the 9/11 terrorists?

On the flip side, **the hurtful action of the heart is** a malicious intent on the part of the person to hurt or control others. Their intent is to get his or her needs met no matter whom they hurt—even if it is members of their own family. An example of this malicious intention is the serial killer John Wayne Gacy. In the 70s, he killed a number of young men and buried their bodies on his own property. This horrific act of brutality not only affected the lives of the victims' families, but Gacy's own family as well.

We must remember, by our unawareness of our pain and our efforts to temporarily mask this pain, we also conceal understanding the source behind our pain. This crucial information is needed to understand the root cause or drive for our and others behaviors as well as the most beneficial way to handle it. It takes time to both come to an understanding of why the pain occurred, and to acquire the skills necessary to work through it. In some instances, the victim(s) may never understand the reasons behind the pain inflicted. This is precisely why God comes to comfort and eventually mend our hurt and brokenness. He is able to bring us to a place of surrender and provides specific relationships alongside us in our time of pain.

In placing our and others sin and hurt on His altar, taking the yoke off of our shoulders and placing it at His feet where it belongs, we come to a place of reassurance, validation, and eventual forgiveness for ourselves and others.

Now that we have an understanding of pain and where it can originate, we must understand the difference between pain and suffering.

Pain versus Suffering

As mentioned earlier, suffering is the ongoing discomfort and the continuous consequence we receive by acting or by living insanely (doing the same thing over and over again expecting a different result). We go round and round, over and over again, refusing to surrender our "control" to others or to painful circumstances. When you think about it, how successful have you been in past attempts at recovery? Only by truly acknowledging our powerlessness and making the decision to be led by God and open to the perspectives of others will we become receptive to new perceptions, viewpoints and or ideas regarding our issues. There is an old saying "If you are in pain, it will lead you to where it hurts." So, in reality, pain is a good thing, not something to avoid and hide from. Healing starts with our acceptance of pain, understanding what the pain is telling you, and how the pain is disrupting your life.

The unresolved pain we cause, and unresolved hurt we experience from others can, and often does, interfere with our plans to succeed in many areas of life. Pain, which is a temporary state, if not understood and worked through will eventually evolve into suffering and distort our self-image, lower self-confidence, skew our perception, and stifle our ability to achieve God's purpose for happiness. Let's look at the components of success and how pain, hurt and eventual suffering can impede it.

Unresolved Hurt and Success

We all are skillful at something, whether it is communicating with others, listening, writing or any other skilled action we have acquired. Skill can be developed with focus, commitment, and persistence on a particular action. Imagine taking our skills and talents, applying them to our pain, hurt, or confusion. The progress, achievement, and freedom experienced would be phenomenal to say the least. Let's imagine we are good at analyzing situations with reason and logic. Imagine using our God-given gift of reason and logic to breakdown our hurt and pain into understandable information in order to see where it came from and how we are behaving because of it.

We can learn to use our skills to be beneficial to others through communicating God's Word so others can be encouraged and strengthened by His message, or we can unknowingly allow our hurt and suffering to redirect our energies and skills to become damaging and destructive to others and to ourselves. A good example of this is the Columbine shootings. Two Columbine high school students, Eric Harris and Dylan Klebold, read about hostage tactics and practiced shooting their semi-automatic weapons months prior to the school shootings. What if they had taken this same effort and intensity and directed it toward a positive action?

It is apparent in their case that unresolved, unexpressed hurt, frustration, and anger were directed into a dysfunctional form of expression.

I know of, have talked to, and have seen many individuals in recovery centers, homeless shelters, on the street, and in jail who are gifted with innate ability, but are inhibited in expressing their God-given talent because of their unresolved pain, hurt, and suffering. It is important to understand that our pain and hurt can either **1)** be a strong motivational force in our pursuit of success **or 2)** It can be a strong inhibiting force that sabotages our achievements through procrastination, fear of achievement or of failure.

Let's look at the great professional football running back, Herschel Walker. As a child growing up in a racist town in Georgia, Herschel was beaten up and bullied. The motivation for Herschel to overcome this painful experience was so great, that he transformed his body from a pudgy kid to a rock-hard, muscled athlete, and redirected his anger onto the football field. Herschel's way of coping with the painful experiences did not stop there. He also developed dissociative identity disorder (also known as multiple personality disorder)—meaning he literally created another personality in order to escape painful reminders of his past.

Herschel is an example of how our pain, if directed in socially acceptable ways, can drive us to achieve. This unconscious drive is often used to compensate for the past pain and trauma we may have endured. The problem that Herschel and other very accomplished or successful people face, is when they have achieved their goals and there are no more accomplishments or objectives to reach, they can no longer cope in the old, familiar way. Often drugs, relationship, health, and legal problems occur and progressively increase if help is not sought.

Another component of success is passion. Passion is defined as, *"a drive to action for inner satisfaction/enjoyment; to compete for a purpose or cause; or achievement of a goal for intrinsic reasons or to meet the needs of self and others."* When we are passionate about something, we will often endure extraordinary circumstances and obstacles to achieve it.

A good example of passion would be the story of Daniel "Rudy" Ruettiger. Rudy was, a young man with minimal football talent, average intelligence, and was physically average. He overcame extraordinary obstacles to both earn a college degree as well as play football for the University of Notre Dame. It was his passion for the game that drove him to achieve his dream that many said could not be done.

In the midst of pain and suffering, it's hard to realize that we do, in fact have a choice: we can allow the unresolved pain and eventual suffering to control our present behaviors, which will ultimately interfere in the expression of our passion. This forces us to abandon the development of our skills and talents, to be used instead in harmful destructive ways or not at all. Or, we can build **mental toughness** and **emotional resilience**, which is the discipline of understanding how our pain and hurt are inhibiting our talent, passion and skill, and learn to push ourselves beyond our emotional, psychological, spiritual pain thresholds. An example of this is when we have thoughts of wanting to give in to unhealthy behaviors, but having the strength not to do so by looking at the potential consequences.

Our pain will trigger us to procrastinate on actions we know we should be doing. We must courageously challenge these messages of surrender and avoidance, in order to resolve this crisis of self.

Our passion, talents and skill development are frequently diminished by shame and other unhealthy core beliefs. **Unhealthy core beliefs** (see Appendix D; Core Beliefs exercise) are inner beliefs unconscious suggestions brought on from painful childhood encounters or circumstances that are self-imposed, perhaps by you or others, as inadequate, unworthy, or a bad person. This type of core belief paints a bleak outlook, it is very difficult to be passionate about something if you don't believe you can achieve it or even deserve to have it.

With this type of belief system, success and goal setting become unimportant. Guilt and shameful beliefs spark acting out behaviors, such as: impulsivity, addiction, depression, and anxiety just to name a few. These behaviors reinforce our poor self-image, which feed our feelings of unworthiness, guilt and shame. We ultimately add to our suffering and pain by abandoning our life's ambitions, goals, or dreams.

If a person is infected with shame, they have great difficulty in self-reflection and self-awareness. This individual uses procrastination, blame shifting, and other avoidances as a dysfunctional means to avoid the "possible" disappointment of failing to succeed and or seeing themselves as a failure. The irony of this harmful method is that by not attempting to achieve, success is never realized which feeds the original shame belief they have and by resisting to challenge their pain and hurt, they stay victimized and in a constant state of suffering.

By making small consistent efforts toward awareness and understanding, there are initial feelings of pain, increased rationalizing of reasons not to change, and procrastination (this is the resistance to change that stops many from healing). These feelings and thoughts are temporary and weaken as the person continues to push forward, building emotional resiliency in the process. This effort reduces the power of shame, and in turn, exposes the hurt and pain. This moves the person to small incremental changes, which increases self-confidence, that's strengthened by overcoming daily obstacles and discomfort.

It is important to examine in more detail the types of pain and suffering we may endure. Traumatic events are forms of pain and are by far the most overlooked and avoided areas of human experience facing us today. I believe at least fifty to seventy percent of individuals who have chronic anxiety, depression, substance abuse, chaotic/problematic relationships and other mental illnesses have witnessed or experienced a traumatic event in their lives.

It is important to look at and understand trauma and how our traumatic experiences are often the source of our pain and harmful behaviors. It is the unconscious catalyst that is currently influencing our lives today.

As caring and loving creations of God, we have showed this quality from time to time, we are also stained with a sinful nature and are constantly under the attack of the "enemy" and by his disciples. Because of our fallibleness and imperfection, we hurt one another in the most horrific of ways. As human beings, we are bound to our mortality and frailty and we cannot escape the uncertainty of this world. We must face the truth of our life, both its potential and its limits, in order to see life for what it is.

Let's start by examining our past and present situations, events, and relationships for trauma. Defining what trauma is in order to see how trauma plays a role in our fashioning and molding our present selves.

I believe a traumatic event can be either **a single experience, or a prolonged or repeating event, that completely overwhelms the individual's ability to cope emotionally and or psychologically with that experience.** The feeling of being overwhelmed can be delayed by weeks or years. Trauma can be caused by a wide variety of events. There is often a violation of the person's boundaries, values, or security about the world and of their human rights, putting the person in a state of extreme confusion and timidity.

Emotional and/or psychological trauma may happen with physical trauma or exist separately from it. **It is not necessary that the person is physically hurt for trauma** to occur. **Just witnessing extreme emotional situations can induce trauma.** Long-term exposure to situations such as extreme poverty, persistent neighborhood crime (shootings, robberies, etc.) or verbal abuse, can be traumatic. However, not everyone who experiences a traumatic event will become traumatized.

There are four common characteristics of trauma:

- it was unexpected;
- it was psychologically/emotionally overwhelming;
- the person was unprepared or unable to cope with it; and
- the person felt there was nothing they could do to prevent or change it.

There are often profound feelings of helplessness or powerlessness that accompany trauma. It is important to understand *it is not the event that determines whether an experience is traumatic, but the subjective experience of that individual.*

Examples of possible traumatic experiences, events, and or situations include:

- Childhood physical, emotional, or sexual abuse, including prolonged or extreme neglect; also, witnessing such abuse inflicted on another child or an adult.

- Experiences and interactions that are perceived as a psychological attack. For example, when a parent, caregiver or close family member invalidates, negates, or dismisses the child's feelings or beliefs.

- Experiencing an event perceived as life-threatening, such as: automobile or other serious accident, a vicious animal attack, being notified of or having a serious medical illness, being a victim of a violent crime or physical assault, witnessing a terrorist attack.

- Adult experiences of sexual assault or rape.

- Experiencing or witnessing physical or psychological torture.

- Soldiers experiences of warfare.

- Stressful occupational experiences such as police work, EMT, or firefighting.

- Living through a natural catastrophe, such as a tornado, tsunami, or severe earthquake.

Reactions to and symptoms of trauma can be varied, and differ in severity from person to person. A traumatized individual may experience one or several of symptoms. After a traumatic experience, a person will re-experience the trauma by the way they cope or by the consequences associated with avoiding the trauma memories. This cycle often leads the person to use alcohol and/or drugs to try to escape the painful feelings produced by the memories.

A person who has trauma repetition is re-experiencing trauma and their associated symptoms. These symptoms are signs that the body and mind are actively struggling to cope with the traumatic experience (either perceived or real). Present triggering situations are similar to past trauma occurrences. In essence, the past comes alive and intrudes upon the present. This intrusion can cause anxiety and other associated emotional/physical problems (i.e. severe migraines are often a psychosomatic symptom of intense stress and or anxiety is induced by an unconscious traumatic experience).

Often, the person can be completely unaware of what these triggers are, and in many cases can recreate the past traumatic events in the present (trauma repetition).

Upsetting memories such as images, thoughts, or flashbacks may haunt the person, and nightmares may be frequent. Insomnia may occur as lurking fears and insecurity keeps the person vigilant and on the lookout for danger, both day and night.

When a person continually re-experiences or is in trauma repetition, the person is prevented from gaining perspective on the experience(s). This can produce a pattern of prolonged periods of acute arousal punctuated by periods of physical and mental exhaustion. According to Dr. Whittfeld, a leading expert on trauma:

> The dissociated traumatic memories may return subtly or overtly and be manifested by any of a variety of physical sensations (somatic memories), images or nightmares, behavioral reenactments, and other symptoms and signs.[9]

There are several common behavior responses to stressful situations: **proactive, reactive, and passive responses.**

- **Proactive responses** include attempts to address and correct a stressor *before* it has a noticeable effect on our lifestyle. **This can be characterized as an avoidance or flight response.** This response may produce pessimistic or negative beliefs, anticipatory anxiety, pre-judging or labeling the person, event or situation in order to avoid

---

[9] Dr. Whittfield.

being hurt or disappointed. The use of coping strategies is prevalent with this type of response such as isolation, substance abuse/dependency or procrastination.

- **Passive response** is often during a perceived traumatic threat **characterized by an indirect emotional numbness or psychological detachment** (i.e. denial, excessive substance usage, psychosis, dissociation/numbing, and minimizing the trauma). There is often a freeze response, along with a combination of defenses and coping strategies involved.

- **Reactive responses** occur *after* the stress and possible traumas have happened, **it is an intentional directed effort**, aimed more at correcting or minimizing the damage of a stressful event (i.e. anger, rage, distractions, or generally a fight or flight response).

Those who are proactive can often overcome stressors, and are more likely to cope well with unexpected situations. On the other hand, those who are more reactive will often experience more noticeable effects from an unexpected stressor. In the case of those who are passive, theses victims are more likely to suffer from long-term traumatic effects and often rely on conscious coping strategies and unconscious defense mechanisms, such as: denial, blame-shifting, procrastination, minimization, etc.

Role of Empathy in Trauma and Recovery

Let's look at how empathy is developed and the impact empathy has on success, pain and recovery. When we are born, we first develop empathy in relationships with other family members, especially with our mother and father. We hurt one another either intentionally or unintentionally. In healthy families, we are shown how our actions are either physically or emotionally hurtful to others though two primary methods:

1. Parents role-play with the children so that they see the effects of their actions from the victim's perspective. This method teaches children to look outside themselves, shifting their focused attention outward instead of remaining inwardly focused. Parents teach their children to change perspectives, which is essential to future efforts at change.

2. Parents enforce consequences for their children's actions and teach them to reflect on what they have done and how it makes them feel about themselves. This again aids in shifting perspective inward to facilitate self-understanding and promotes confidence in future decision-making. Healthy parents help their children link the skill of empathy or emotional perception shifting, to their actions, and the impact on relationships they have now and will have later in life.

Empathy is a balanced perceptional shift to another person to see life from their point of view. However, when a person places too much emphasis on meeting others needs before their own, this is no longer empathy, this becomes manipulation—when we try to be accepted by others to avoid feeling rejected. It is an attempt by the manipulator to control others emotional reactions because it makes the manipulator feel uncomfortable.

Generally in dysfunctional families, the parents or primary caregiver struggle to step outside of their own needs and are unable to teach or model empathy to their own children, the children grow up detached from their parents. They can become inwardly focused on meeting their own needs and wants or outward focused concerned more about the needs of others than themselves. These children struggle in properly shifting perspectives—either unable to empathize with others, or unable to focus on meeting their own important needs. Often, these children have been so neglected and hurt by those significant others they are traumatized, therefore, are in survival mode. They are driven to get their needs met regardless of how it hurts others. They also struggle with seeing how their actions will result in future negative consequences or have little forethought.

According to Maslow's Hierarchy of Needs, there are five levels of needs: *Biological/Physiological; Safety; Relational; Self-Esteem; and Self-Fulfillment.* We cannot go onto the next level until we have acquired our current level of needs. For instance, if an addict struggles to eat healthfully and get a restful night's sleep (Level 1), how can they expect to be motivated to get or maintain a job (Level 4) or to be responsible for themselves or others (Level 3)?

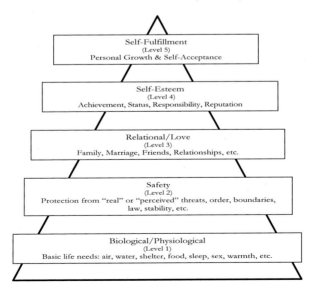

Self-Fulfillment
(Level 5)
Personal Growth & Self-Acceptance

Self-Esteem
(Level 4)
Achievement, Status, Responsibility, Reputation

Relational/Love
(Level 3)
Family, Marriage, Friends, Relationships, etc.

Safety
(Level 2)
Protection from "real" or "perceived" threats, order, boundaries, law, stability, etc.

Biological/Physiological
(Level 1)
Basic life needs: air, water, shelter, food, sleep, sex, warmth, etc.

If our current levels of needs are being met, we can proceed to the next level. However, past and present hurt, pain, fear, and trauma can stop us from moving forward and upward. If a lower level need must be met (i.e. if a national disaster occurs), we will revert to behaviors to meet our basic needs). As we reflect on the Word of God, he brings us assurance, comfort, and ways to righteously meet our personal needs, while empathizing, and helping others in achieving their needs as well.

In the case of the addict, his/her life is filled with the pain of broken relationships, feelings of emptiness and mistrust of others. By not meeting their current needs, they will struggle with developing empathy. The addict will continue to be in "survival mode," only caring about his or her basic needs being met. Without empathy, the person stays in the cycle of continuous suffering, dysfunction and egocentric delusion.

By recreating or revisiting the origin of the trauma under psychologically safe conditions, we achieve the process of healing the trauma. When trauma is revisited, it can bring about healthy change in how people perceive themselves, their relationships, as well as their philosophical, spiritual, or religious viewpoint from a mature adult perspective.

To gain essential understandings and the freedom from traumatic memories, we must examine how we were affected by certain events. We might remember times of stupidity, family fights, relationship struggles, addictions, infidelities still held in secret, memories of our parents' divorce, or back to a time of sexual, emotional, or physical abuses that dominated home life.

Tools to Use

1. Life history exercise: write a detailed account of incidents of painful traumatic memories and experiences. Starting from your earliest memories to the present.
2. Journal daily about experiences, relationships and events that trigger traumatic memories.
3. It is best to seek out a trained professional counselor in order to work through reoccurring intense memories of abuse or other traumatic experiences.

Key Point

It takes energy to suppress energy. Emotion is a form of energy. The energy that could be used for emotional expression, self-awareness, and building relationships or to advert from making poor decisions is instead allocated to create a public mask, manipulate and hide our fear. Only by true genuine expression of painful emotions, crippling thoughts, and contrasting beliefs can we address the relational issues that traumatic pain has inhibited for so long. In order to know ourselves, we must have and hang on to the hope that with every obstacle we overcome, there are rewards that we gain.

In a nutshell, by first understanding we are not where we want to be in life, we can then embrace the reality of being lost in the quagmire of emotional confusion, pain, suffering, and shame either through the actions of others or either due to our own short sightedness.

Questions to Ponder

1. Do you have disturbing persistent memories? If so, please describe it in great detail.
2. How do you specifically avoid, escape or distract yourself from painful emotions, people or life situations?
3. Looking back to your childhood, what occurred to you to cause you to feel, think or act the way you do today?
4. How do you believe others see you?
5. How do you see others?
6. How do you wish to be seen by others?
7. Were you ever a victim because of the actions of someone else?
8. What pain have you caused others?

8

The Gift of Forgiveness

"To forgive is to set a prisoner free and the discovery that
the prisoner was you."

— Lewis B. Smedes

"Bear with each other and forgive whatever grievances you
may have against one another. Forgive as the Lord forgave
you."

— Colossians 3:13

In this chapter, we will discuss what forgiveness is and what it is not. I will outline in detail the process of forgiveness and how forgiveness releases us from suffering and puts us on the road to harmony of mind and spirit. We have all been the victim of or have been the perpetrator of hurt, betrayal, abuse or lies. Because of our sinful nature, we prey upon others and we have been preyed on.

God has given us a way out of this predatory cycle, free from being used, abused, and controlled by the sins of others. When it comes to healing the wounds we put on others or what has been placed on us. The Word tells us in Psalm 103:12 (commentary):

'As far as the east is from the west, so far has he removed our transgression from us.' East and west can never meet, this symbolic portrait of God's forgiveness when he forgives our sin he separates it from us and doesn't even remember it. We never wallow in the past for God forgives and forgets. We tend to dredge up the ugly past but God has wiped our record clean. If we are to follow God we must model his forgiveness. When we forgive another we must also forgive the sin. Otherwise we have not truly forgiven.

It is crucial to understand how forgiveness can break us free from past shame, regret and hostility that controls us and keeps us from enjoying life and receiving the love we richly deserve. It is important to understand how this pain controls us and how to appropriately express our hurt through the forgiveness process.

The Power of Forgiveness

I remember seeing a program on television of an elderly couple whose only son was killed during a convenience store robbery. The son was working during the summer to earn money for college. The young man's murderer netted $80 dollars total from the robbery. The robber was caught several months later and went to trial. Over the next two years, the trial was postponed several times. In that time, the father passed away before the actual trial and eventual conviction of the robber occurred. The mother of the young man attended every court appearance.

Ten years had passed since the robber's conviction and sentencing to life in prison without the possibility of parole. The victim's mother asked to speak with the man who killed her son. The prisoner's hands and feet were hand cuffed; he was tattooed from head to toe with the hardest non-emotional look you would ever see. The prisoner had a long history of criminal behavior and he grew up in an abusive home. The prisoner was escorted by several prison guards and then seated in an interview room. The mother came in with the assistance of a walker; you could see that the years of pain and hurt had taken its toll on this woman physically.

The mother placed a picture of her son on the desk and sat down and began to tell the prisoner about her son and of his hopes of being a pediatrician. She spoke of the failed attempts to conceive a child as a young woman and how God had eventually blessed her with her son.

As this frail elderly woman spoke to the prisoner, telling him of the enormous pain and suffering he had caused her and her now deceased husband because of his actions. The camera showed the prisoner transform from indifference to sadness and regret. The prisoner's tough exterior began to melt away like ice on a hot summer day. The prisoner's indifferent gaze soon turned into shame and sorrow for what he had done. The mother stated to the prisoner, "You have taken everything from me, but you will no longer control me…I have thought and prayed long and hard, I forgive you for what you have done to me and I give you to my Father in Heaven." The mother stood up, took her picture and confidently walked out of the room.

The prisoner sat there with his head down and a stream of tears rolling down his face. The program fast-forwarded to five years later. The mother of the victim had died. The prisoner had become a Christian and had started a prison ministry that focused on forgiveness and helping victims of violent crimes in the healing process.

Forgiveness is a powerful means to resolve past hurts and pain by releasing those from a debt they can never pay. The forgiveness process, if done in a particular way and with a sincere heart, can bring untold freedom to those imprisoned in the chains of anger, hurt, and betrayal. I will explain the process of forgiveness and discuss what it is and is not. First, let's talk about what it means to forgive.

What Forgiveness Is and Is Not

Is forgiveness an absence of pain inflicted by the offender? Is it letting someone get away with the offense? Is it a means to forget what happened? Does the relationship have to return to the way it was before the offense for there to be true forgiveness? Or as Christians are we expected to place the offender back into a position of trust they once had before? There are so many ideas about what forgiveness is and is not and it is often misunderstood.

Myth: If the offender "suffers," this will make everything better!

Reality: *Forgiveness is defined as releasing someone from a debt they cannot pay.* It is an unconditional pardon from restitution for an offense commented against you. What we did to someone or what was done to us is in the past and can never be undone. We cannot go back in time and change what occurred. The reality is, no matter how much we want the offender to suffer for what they have done to us or to a loved one, and nothing will change what happened.

When an offender receives consequences for their actions, either having to pay out monies, replacing items lost or destroyed, or going to jail, they are committing acts of restitution; however, there are other underlying effects of the offender's actions that are not tangible and cannot be erased by the offender themselves. For instance, when a spouse is unfaithful in a marriage, the unfaithful spouse may apologize profusely and do everything they can to rectify the relationship, which is a positive thing; however, there will remain underlying thoughts and feelings of mistrust, anger, and apprehension with the hurt spouse until they reach a place of forgiveness.

Myth: You can forgive and forget.

Reality: *Forgiveness is not forgetting the offense, who offended you,* or *how it affected you.* The cliché "To forgive and forget" is a lie used to induce denial and self-deception (to alleviate the pain of memory). First of all, I have never heard of a person who can induce amnesia at will! Forgiveness is the exact opposite, it is a conscious effort in using our focused attention, self-awareness, honesty, and persistence in examining the past offense(s) from top to bottom, from side to side and all around, so it no long remains a mystery like a splinter in our soul, festering and eventually poisoning our lives.

Myth: Forgiveness is a feeling.

Reality: *Forgiveness is not a feeling.* If you think about it, to forgive someone or ask for forgiveness is a painful **action**. If we had to wait until we felt comfortable, then many of us would never decide to forgive. *Forgiveness is a decision we come to after much prayer, reflection on our pain and acceptance of the offense's effect on our lives.* The decision to forgive is made before we choose to forgive. Forgiveness is a process that starts with a decision that you make. Forgiveness is a choice that is made with no motive in getting anything return. Forgiveness is a choice not to continue to allow the past offense(s) to control your thoughts, feelings and behaviors. The bible offers forgiveness as both freedoms from hurts' enslavement and offering obedience to the will of God (forgiveness is an example of living in God's will, which results in freedom).

Myth: Forgiveness is restoring the relationship back to the way it was.

Reality: *Forgiveness is not reconciliation!* Forgiveness is not about fixing the relationship to what it was. You are not trying to be a friend or continuing a relationship as it once was. Forgiveness is about breaking free from the control another's actions have on you. Asking for forgiveness is about breaking free from the guilt, hurt and taking responsibility for your actions. It is not about the victim accepting you and forgiving you right then and there. Reconciliation is the process of mending a relationship; it takes two. Forgiveness takes only one person, that person is YOU.

Myth: Forgiveness should be given and asked for at the time of the offense.

Reality: *Forgiveness is a decision and any sincere decision is thought out and examined carefully before it is expressed.* Often we hear someone who has been hurt, forgive the person who hurt him or her quickly. This "quickie" forgiveness is frequently said in order to move on from an uncomfortable situation that both the offender and victim find themselves in. This glancing over the situation is an avoidance strategy that keeps the situation unresolved. It is important to build relationships on trust and honesty regarding the others role in the offense and how it "hurt" you and vice versa.

It is okay to tell the other that you have thought about the incident and its effects. It is also okay not to forgive the person right away. A true and sincere extension of, or request for, forgiveness will take time to decide. Some offenders who ask for forgiveness may never receive an answer, some offenders may (if not careful) receive a bullet in their behind. We will discuss ways to communicate to those we have hurt later in this chapter.

The Process of Forgiveness

Forgiveness is a process, and like any process in life, there are steps to truly forgive. We will examine these steps in detail and discover how forgiveness promotes healing. You must **first** decide to forgive the person who offended you or seek forgiveness for offending others. **Second,** understand the offense in question (How were you offended? Or, how did you offend the other?). **Third,** identify who offended you or whom you offended. What was their or your responsibility in the offense? **Fourth,** describe the circumstances and events surrounding the offense. **Fifth,** what were the thoughts and feelings before, during and after the offense? **Finally,** how did the offense affect you and or how do you believe the offense hurt the other person?

1. Make the decision to forgive or to ask for forgiveness.

As mentioned earlier, take time to reflect on yourself and see if you are currently carrying hurt, anger, or any other pain from the actions of others in your past. Are you holding onto guilt, shame, or remorse from your past behaviors that have hurt innocent others? To decide to forgive others or to be forgiven is deciding to finally be free and to give the gift of forgiveness to others.

2. How were you offended? Or how did you offend the other?

Describe specifically how you were hurt: "Cousin Johnny embezzled thousands of dollars from the family business and it lead to us filing bankruptcy." Or how you offend others by your actions? "I had intercourse with Jane Doe when she was passed out from a night of drinking heavily…I know she would have never wanted to have sex with me…I raped her plain and simple."

3. Identify the person who was offended by your actions or the person who hurt you by their actions.

If known, name them or their relation to you (i.e. cousin "Johnny" or "Billy" the sixteen-year-old kid who lived in my neighborhood or describe them if you don't know them).

Denial plays a huge part in derailing this step. Denial often occurs when the offense comes from a family member, an authority figure, or someone very close. We will rationalize their actions and ours in order to avoid seeing the offense for what it is…hurtful.

Avoidance is also a way to preserve the relationship (the fantasy bond we talked about in chapter 3), much like a child will endure abuse to maintain their connection to their caregiver or parent. It is critical to be honest with yourself and see the relationship for what it is and not what you want it to be.

4. It is important to look at what was your responsibility (if any) you had in the incident.

Did you provoke the situation, person or event? Did you report it or conceal it from the proper authorities or persons in charge? Are you taking on more of the responsibility then what is yours? Are you putting off your responsibility onto others? I had a client whose husband (primary provider) would verbally abuse her, even in front of their children, friends or his co-workers. In a later session, she told me, "I know he's stressed about what is going on at his job…I know he doesn't mean what he says or how he says it."

5. Describe in detail the offense(s) that hurt you or the way(s) in which you hurt others.

Describe the circumstances that surrounded the offense(s): What lead up to the offense? Where did it happen? Did it occur in a bedroom, garage, or at a concert?

How did it happen? At a party? Was there a lot of drinking or drug abuse occurring? When did it occur? What were the sights, smells, and sounds of the environment? Describe what you observed taking place. What were your actions and the actions of others?

6. Describe your thoughts and feelings surrounding the offense.

In the forgiveness process, it is important to bring forth awareness to how you felt and thought before, during, and after the offense. **Before the offense:** I felt **secure** and **comfortable** when Cousin Johnny took over as CFO of the family business. I believed in him and trusted he would do a good job. **During the offense:** I felt **anxious, troubled,** and **confused** when I noticed problems with the spreadsheets and amount of money in the accounts. I did not even suspect Johnny; he would never do anything dishonest to the family. **After the offense:** I felt **shocked, betrayed,** and **enraged** when I heard Johnny embezzled thousands of dollars from our business to support his drug habit.

7. How did the offense affect you or others you offended?

Describe the spiritual, physical, psychological, and emotional effects of the offense on you? Or how it affected others? How did the offense alter your view of yourself, others, or God? How has the offense changed the way you or they behave, feel or think? "I believe Jane Doe will never trust me or men ever again after I took advantage of her while she was passed out drunk…she may be worried she received a sexually transmitted disease from me or even got pregnant." It is a good idea to ask a close, trustworthy friend or relatives if they notice any changes in your attitude, behaviors, or mood.

After we have gone over each of the above steps, write down your thoughts and feelings, answering each question and any other questions you may have. When we have come to the decision to truly forgive, *there is no set amount of time it takes to go through this process.* It may take days, weeks or up to decades to complete this process. We can now proceed to conveying our gift of forgiveness or asking for it.

When forgiving another, it is best to do it face-to-face. If face-to-face is not possible (due to distance or a death), a phone call is better than a letter; a letter is better than nothing at all. *Forgiveness should be done when it is reasonable and safe to do so.* We do not want to meet face-to-face with someone who is violent or harmful by ourselves. It should also not be forced, when emotions are high, or surprising the person at their home unannounced.

If known, you can call or email the offender or offended person to meet in order to discuss the relationship and issues within it. Upon meeting them, ask them politely to just listen until you are finished. You can express your answer to the following:

- **What was their responsibility and yours in the offense?**
- **How they hurt you or how you believe you hurt them.**
- **How the offense has currently impacted you.**
- **How the offense made you feel.**
- **Express your forgiveness for their actions or ask for forgiveness for your actions.**

The most important aspect of forgiveness, whether giving it or asking for it, is that it is not conditional. The gift of forgiveness is not based on how they react or respond to the request. Remember that forgiveness is for you in releasing you from bondage and self-persecution. It is not dependent on the other person's receiving or rejecting it. For instance, if asking for forgiveness and the offended person tells you to go to hell and walks away from you, this does not diminish the value that asking for forgiveness has on you and its impact on setting you free.

In the event you are offering forgiveness to someone who is deceased, forgiveness can be done in a form of a letter to that person. The letter outlines the above format to the offender and the statement, "I forgive you and place you in the hands of my Heavenly Father," should end the letter. You can read the letter aloud to close family and friends, and either burn the letter or bury it as a symbolic gesture of letting go of the control the pain has had on you.

Myth: After I forgive or ask for forgiveness, I should no longer feel the pain of the offense.

Reality: *You will continue to feel the feelings associated with the offense and the offender.* These are called "residual feelings." The feelings should not be as intense as they were prior to the beginning of the forgiveness process. The difference between the feelings before and the residual feelings are in how the feelings of the offense before forgiveness has controlled you, where the residual feelings are felt, but are not so intense that they dominate and alter your life. Over time, the memories and feelings will continue to subside.

Tools to Use

1. Look up scriptural references regarding forgiveness and contemplate on what the Word says about it.
2. Pray for the strength to forgive or asking to be forgiven.
3. Answer the "Questions to Ponder" at the end of the chapter.

Key Point

The decision to forgive someone or to ask for forgiveness is one of the most decisive and empowering actions a person can take toward healing that is available. Forgiveness is so biblically sound and fundamental that Jesus taught on it and demonstrated forgiveness throughout His ministry. Forgiveness should never be taken lightly or causally.

It's a remarkable power that comes from our God given ability to self-reflect on ourselves, bringing our hurt and pain to self-awareness where it loses its grip on us when this understanding is applied, dealing with it (examination and understanding of it) and lastly, to cast it out from our lives. God has clearly given us the Way to be free and thrive despite our past and our current situation in life.

Questions to Ponder

1. Who do you need to forgive or ask for their forgiveness?
2. What has you hesitate about forgiving or asking for it?
3. What are you holding onto that requires forgiveness?
4. What are your consequences for not seeking forgiveness or giving it?
5. How will forgiveness set you free?

9

Who Speaks for Tomorrow?

"Yesterday is but Today's memory, and Tomorrow is Today's dream."

– Khalil Gibran

"Know also that wisdom is sweet to your soul; if you find it there is a future hope for you, and your hope will not be cut off."

– Proverbs 24:14

As we conclude, or is it the beginning of self-discovery and understanding? Will our tomorrows be the same as our yesterdays? What kind of life do we choose? Will it be a life filled with struggles, worry, depression and uncertainty? Or a life filled with true relationships, optimism and confidence about the future, comforted by God's grace and blessing? By picturing the type of tomorrows we want, this gives us something to go for, an idealized, but realistic future to achieve.

God promises a life of abundance and joy, through His Word we will live as He intended for us to live. So, who speaks for us? Who speaks about the past or our futures? The Lord our God speaks to us, about us and for us. He also speaks to us through life events, situations, and especially through various acquaintances, family and friends. It is vital that we become disciplined in what I call "contemplative stillness." This type of stillness is stillness free of our selfish worries, wants, and needs. It is an intentional focus on God and His daily messages to us through these situations and it is in our application of that divine message that moves us into the path of recovery. There are several key questions to ask ourselves:

1. What is God telling me through my present situation, event, or current relationship?
2. How is the "enemy" distorting God's message for me in my present circumstance?
3. How can I apply the above knowledge and understanding to my life and relationships?

In order to achieve true self-understanding we must consultant our Creator. Think about it, if you accidentally poked yourself in the eye with a salad fork would you go to a plumber? An optomologist? If one morning you looked in the mirror and your hair looks like a complete mess, would you go to a florist or hairstylist to fix it? Of course, you would go to the appropriate individual with the right knowledge, skills, and experience to fix your problem. So, if we are confused about life, its purpose, and meaning, shouldn't we go to our Creator for the answers? We are kidding ourselves if we believe we can find God's messages, purpose, and meaning through the material things of this world. We must learn God's most wonderful gift; a gift that brings us in touch with our past, our present and waits for us in the future, so who speaks for you and I? The gift I am referring to is free will, the freedom to choose to follow or not to follow God; the freedom to decide the course of our lives and what we chose to include or exclude in it.

In counseling, I cannot and would not try to force anyone into a choice or action. Ultimately, it is their decision to make. The Word states:

> I guide you in the way of wisdom and lead you along straight paths. When you walk, your steps will not be hampered; when you run, you will not stumble. Hold on to instruction; do not let it go; guard it well, for it is your life.
>
> – Proverbs 4:11-13

As we learn to make important life decisions, we must reach out and learn from those who are able to apply wisdom, understanding and clarity. Who speaks for the unwise, closed-minded, and stubborn individual? I believe they speak for themselves and only for themselves. For instance, I counseled a young man who stated his intention to change, but applied very little effort on his own to see that change happened. The young man's mother called me very distraught about the path her twenty-something-year-old son was headed down. She stated to me, "What are **we** going to do about this." I then stated back to the mom (of course being sensitive to her feelings) and said, "Nothing. *We* aren't going to do a thing." I heard nothing over the phone but stunned silence.

I explained to mom the importance of this young man making good choices, but first, he had to decide on his own to seek help. She and I talked about setting appropriate boundaries, encouragement versus enabling. We discussed what God's purpose was for this young man and how this young man would appreciate his efforts more if he chose the path of recovery for himself and not have others choose for him.

I explained to the mom that making choices for him sends the message that he is neither trustworthy nor capable of making choices for himself. This keeps him dependent on others. In other words, he remains a child that needs to be taken care of. There are times when we are forced to take action for loved ones who struggle with making rational choices. This scenario is not one of them.

When we learn how God speaks to us, this brings us under His authority. We learn we are now able to speak for ourselves, communicating to others with grace and empathy. We begin to see the world through the spiritual filter of the Word and not through our distorted filter of hurt and pain. We learn to speak with honesty, authenticity and with confident genuineness.

Let's have a detailed look at the process of healing and what God says about this process. The Word speaks about healing and change quite a bit:

> "And God is able to make all grace abound to you, so that in all things at all times, having all that you need, you will abound in every good work."
>
> – 2 Corinthians 9:8

> "You were taught, with regard to your former way of life, to put off your old self, which is being corrupted by its deceitful desires; to be made new in the attitude of your minds; and to put on the new self, created to be like God in true righteousness and holiness."
>
> – Ephesians 4:22-24

God is a God of process, not of quick solutions, astrology, ointments, pills, or quick remedies. By living in accordance to God's Word, we express the following character traits that enhance and make positive change permanent: Patience, persistence, perseverance, consistency, discipline, confidence; these leave us with a sense of wholeness.

By giving in to our old selves and continuing to resist the process of change. We send the message to others and God, "I speak for me; I don't need or want you." When we blindly and arrogantly speak for ourselves, we will exhibit following characteristics: impatience, indecisiveness, desperately pursuing temporary gratifications, inconsistencies, insecurities, impulsivities, uncertainty, feelings of unworthiness.

To transform from arrogantly speaking on our own behalf; letting go of our perceived control and allowing God to speak for us, so we can eventually speak for ourselves glorifying His Holy name. The process involves leaving the old and moving into the new. We will discuss this renewal or process of change continuum in detail.

Process of Change

In every stage of life, there is a process. Whether physical, spiritual or psychological, the process of healing can be quick in some areas and slow in others. The speed of healing and change depends on the individual's personality traits, support system, life situation and or intellectual capacity. This process is similar to the stages of grief because we are mourning a loss. We are in mourning of our old life, even as painful and dysfunctional as it was, it was familiar and allowed us to handle past painful circumstances (in an immature and distorted way).

It is important to understand the process of change and the stages of healing in order to see where we are in the process. We will examine each stage of the healing process.

1. **Denial:** A stage in which we experience a numbed disbelief of reality. This stage is the most difficult to penetrate because it assists us in coping with overwhelming emotional and psychological pain we experienced daily. We use a variety of conscious (coping strategies) and unconscious (defenses) methods to buffer experiencing hurt and other discomfort. Often the person is unaware of these defenses; they have relied on them most of their life.

2. **Objectivity:** Individuals who suffer with relational problems and other mental health issues often lack objectivity in seeing the severity of their problems. Objectivity helps in two ways. **First,** it helps to reduce our emotionality, allowing people to think more rationally. **Second,** objectivity provides a neutral territory that allows for a panoramic point of view into ourselves and allows a less bias view of who we are to take place.

3. **Bargaining:** Trying to hang on to old behaviors, attitudes and beliefs without experiencing the past and present pain and suffering it caused. (i.e. I'll go to counseling, If I can still smoke marijuana). Bargaining is making "some" changes without truly changing the lifestyle that has caused so many problems.

4. **Anger:** Feelings we experience for the actions of others or what we have done to place ourselves in our current situation or the realization of what was lost. For example, we may be angry with ourselves for the amount of money, relational trust or opportunity lost because of our behaviors, attitudes or beliefs.

5. **Grief:** The loss—sorrow—of what once was—the snapshots of past pleasures of our old life—and the

realization of where we are currently in life (i.e. feeling remorse for the problems we caused others by our actions. For instance: a husband will feel ashamed and regretful because his drinking forced his wife to divorce him). Grief has no length of time or method. *Grief is a way to express inner sadness and regret in an appropriate way.*

6. **ACCEPTANCE**: The final stage of healing. Acceptance is the feeling of contentment and having a realistic understanding of how one got to where they are in life, the losses along the way, the blessings acquired and what is needed in order to appropriately deal with their current problems in a mature and Godly manner. The individual has learned to express their inner selves and know where they go from "here."

The most valued aspect of healing is in trusting God's process and submitting to that process. In surrendering to Him, we are receptive to a plan of healing that surpasses our expectations and understanding of ourselves. Initially, we feel vulnerable and out of control, but ironically, we are cradled and protected by our Heavenly Father; gradually gaining confidence in ourselves along the way. We will look at several key factors of this process and how it coincides with change.

Effort is one of two key components of the Healing process; Effort is the intentional action(s) used during the healing process. It is the consistent drive to understand God's purpose for the individual, simultaneously, the individual gains understanding of self. Effort consists of repetitive work, actions and the acquiring of skills, abilities and knowledge applied daily in order to create new and lasting responses, instead of relying on dysfunctional habits and reactionary behaviors. The Word speaks on effort quite well:

"Go to the ant, you sluggard; consider its ways and be wise! It has no commander, no overseer or ruler, yet it stores its provisions in summer and gathers its food at harvest. How long will you lie there, you sluggard? When will you get up from your sleep? A little sleep, a little slumber, a little folding of the hands to rest—and poverty will come on you like a bandit and scarcity like an armed man."

— Proverbs 6:6-11

"The way of the sluggard is blocked with thorns, but the path of the upright is a highway."

— Proverbs 15:19

Let's face it! Doing nothing does nothing for you! You can remain hoping the suffering stops or passes you by, which is self-deception, or you can see the suffering for what it is and work the process toward restoration.

Time is the second component; Time is God's secret ingredient in the process of healing. Think about it, wine is better when the aging process in incorporated. A tiny seed can have all the water, sunlight, and food it needs, but without time, nothing occurs. Time is important in a number of ways:

1. As time passes, we are able to look back at past mistakes and victories in order to learn and make present adjustments and changes for a better future. Where we focus our attention (past, present, or future) will show others and ourselves

what we value most, i.e. if we live in the past we suffer regret, remorse, and shame.

2. If we stay in the present, we become lost in instant gratification and survival or too much in the future, we become fortunetellers, "What if this or that?" We are then stricken by anxiety or preoccupied with worry. Time is God's gift to us. It gives us a scale of understanding by asking, "How is the past intruding on our present and how will our present, if not changed, become our future?"

3. Time brings about clarity as to how our pain is showing itself and to the most effective way to address it; time allows us the ability to hone our skills and to familiarize our self with the new change. We then cast a vision to who we want to be despite where we came from.

"Humble yourselves, therefore, under God's mighty hand, that He may lift you up in due time. Cast all your anxiety on Him because He cares for you."

– 1 Peter 5: 6-7

So, when we combine both the decisiveness of effort with the patience and constancy of time, the Word assures us that we will "reap what we sow" and our efforts and the time we invest are all proportional to the results we obtain. The process of healing is by no means a passive position or comfortable one. It takes diligence and perseverance in order to achieve the results you want.

The path from here to serenity is filled with uncertainty, struggle, and pain. However, the path from here to serenity is also filled with understanding, joy, confidence, love, purpose, and change. It is the quest for healing that beckons our struggles to come forth. The renewing and rebuilding comes with breaking walls down. This is the essence of restoration, the consistent move to be better than before, genuinely embracing where we came from and boldly declaring, *"I will not remain a slave to sin!"* *"I will not let my behaviors and past sins define me!"* and *"I will make a positive change today, with God's help!"*

This is God's plan for you and me—to authentically connect with others while unapologetically accepting our imperfections in the process. By our sacrifices and willingness to change, we are able to pour into the lives of others along our journey and by those efforts, we glorify our Father in Heaven.

> "Thank you Lord, for bringing us to this point in our lives, strengthening and comforting us along the way with Your Word, wisdom and understanding. Strengthen us to be of courage and resolve Oh Lord, May all of our sacrifices, pains and triumphs Glorify Your Eternal name. Praise be to You Heavenly Father and Your Son Jesus Christ! Forever."

Appendix A

Emotions Defined

As discussed in earlier chapters, feelings are physiological (body sensational) or responses to outside events, situations and people. While emotions are labels or ways we identify those feelings *(i.e. tension in the neck and extremities, fast heart rate, and deep breathing (body sensations) may be labeled as anger, hostility or fear)*.

The average human is capable of experiencing 1,500 different emotions. All of these emotions are God-given and God does not make mistakes, nor does He create feelings/emotions just to annoy us! Feelings and emotions are essential in helping us do three important things:

1. To connect with one another;
2. In understanding a situation(s) we encounter and what it currently means to us (based on the value we place on them and past experiences);
3. Feelings/Emotions assist in survival by overriding our thoughts (which are slower than feelings) for quick lifesaving responses in certain events, *i.e. swerving out of the way of an oncoming car in the road.*

Emotions are like colors. There are the primary colors red, blue, and yellow, which represent general emotions such as mad, sad, glad, and happy. These surface emotions do not tell anything specific about what is going on inside of a person. However, like the primary colors, emotions are made up of combinations of other emotions and those emotions tell a more specific tale of what the person is going through and how they perceive their world.

It is crucial for individuals to develop a way of expressing their inner feelings and emotions to others. By doing so, this averts us from many unnecessary explosive behaviors such as fighting, breaking or punching walls or doors, yelling, and other out of control behaviors. It also minimizes and/or eliminates "acting in" behaviors such as self-harming behaviors, depression, isolation, substance abuse, and suicides.

Using the format "I feel (or felt)...about...because..." is a great tool for expressing your inner self to others. This avoids misunderstandings and unresolved hurt(s).

I felt or feel... (Identify the emotions or feelings)
About... (Describe the situation, event or person)
Because... (Describe the reasons you felt or feel this way about the situation event or person)

An example:

*I felt **annoyed** yesterday,*
*about **you not take out the trash last night**,*
*because **I had to take it out myself this morning and I was late for work.***

When our emotions are explored they can reveal a richness and produce an insightful look at how the person is experiencing life. When I hear someone say I'm fine, good, okay, etc. this tells me a number of things: 1) words like "fine," "good," and "okay" are not emotions; they are

124

general descriptors. Such as: "my job is going okay," or "it was good to see her again." These words say very little to others about how the person truly feels. However, using the "I feel...about...because..." format that was previously discussed, we can understand more clearly the speakers thoughts and feelings. For instance:

I feel *confident*
About *my position at work*
Because *my supervisor told me what an excellent job I am doing*

Or

I was *excited*
About *seeing her again*
Because *she has encouraged and supported me for years.*

The two examples above definitely articulate the speaker emotions and thoughts to the listener in a way where there is no mystery, misperception or lack of understanding in what the speaker is experiencing. This type of communication sends the message of trust and openness. The listener is now more open to expressing him or herself as well.

Appendix B

Deception Cycle

We all see the world in our own way, our perceptions are based on our past experiences and the "worldly" approaches we chose to use in handling events, relationships and situations. We all use deception in one way or another to navigate our world. Deception helps to buffer the harshness of reality. Deception protects our sense of self (ego), as well as, helping to get our needs meet. However, when the frequency and intensity in the use of deception increases, this will pose significant social, relational and other problems in the individual. It is important to understand that the longer the deception continues (gaining dependency on it) the greater the gap is from reality. Eventually, it becomes too great of a gap causing psychological break or we may use some other means to aid in bridging this gap like TV, drugs, alcohol, sex etc. Below is the deception cycle. Like any cycle, the conditions must be right. For this particular cycle, shame or some negative core belief is formed from an early childhood trauma/painful experience (root cause).

1. **Shame based beliefs take root**

Shame based beliefs are formed from painful early life experiences; the early shame is perpetuated and strengthened by acting on our destructive behaviors. It is the added consequences of the destructive behaviors that add even more regret and shame on top of the original shaming beliefs.

2. **Self-deception:**

Are conscious and unconscious methods employed to maintain the illusion of control and to protect our sense of self (ego) such as: denial, rationalizing, blame-shifting, etc.

3. **The drive to deceive others is equal to the need to be deceived by others**

The deceivers try to convince others to go along with their actions or beliefs. When they get others to buy in on their lifestyle, in their mind, this legitimizes their actions, thus they continue to deceive themselves into believing their actions are somehow "acceptable." For instance: they will get others to use drugs with them or to support/ignore their behaviors (enablers). The old saying, "Misery loves company" could not be truer in this stage.

4. **Develops a distorted view of reality**

"If I can be what my parents want me to be, they will love and accept me"; "I can't do anything right!" or "I can handle my drug use, my brain make up is different than other drug addicts." These distorted beliefs and attitudes are adopted in an attempt to bridge the gap between the deceiver's true chaotic circumstances and dysfunctional lifestyle with their unrealistic/distorted views of reality. Deceivers also tend to focus on changing others and their surroundings instead of changing themselves. This lack of self -reflection maintains their distorted view.

5. **The person receives increased consequences, which worsens their circumstances further**

Despite repeated pleas by family and friends, jail, fines and other consequences, they are determined to alter the unchangeable reality. They manipulate others to get want they want, instead of changing themselves and seeing their circumstances realistically. This continued delusion of control produces greater consequences and more anguish. The deceiver becomes more deceived and increasingly more focused on changing their circumstances in the old way, which is what got them into their present predicament in the first place. "They are in fact, throwing gasoline into a raging fire."

6. **Constant and increasing efforts to deceive others and self by lying, rationalizing, secrets, manipulation, threats, etc., to maintain distorted view of reality**

They struggle to let go of "control" despite the crushing consequences of reality all around them. They continue both psychological (denial, blame shifting, minimizing and playing the victim) and physical (drugs, alcohol, sex, etc.) methods in order to divert responsibility from themselves and onto others. They might say,
"The police are out to get me!"
"If my family would have only…"
"I wouldn't have done it if not for…"

7. **Desperate attempts to fit distorted view with reality**

There are more intense and riskier behaviors in a vain attempt to maintain some familiarity, predictability and control. The deceived continue to affiliate themselves with like-minded, unsafe persons; this increases the frequency and amount of drug use, escaping/avoiding behaviors in order to cope with present chaotic circumstances.

8. **The cycle starts all over again**

Shameful beliefs, perceptions, attitudes about self, others and God are reinforced and intensified by continued consequences impulsive behaviors, poor decisions and harmful relationships. Stress increases and the person continues to rely on ineffective, harmful reactions to current situations.

Appendix C

Relational and Family Drama Triangle

Below are the relational roles most encountered within and out of the family. Learn these roles well. It will not be long before you can identify others in these roles and the manipulative dynamic that occurs. Ask yourself "what role(s) do I assume?" and "In which relationship do I assume it?" *Remember, these are unconscious roles; many of the relationships we are currently in are based on one or more of these roles. We are generally attracted to one another because we play a role that meets both our needs and the needs of our partners (i.e. The Victims will seek the Rescuers for caring and attention while The Placater will seek the Hero for acceptance and approval).

The Victim often utters phrases like: "Help me," "Poor me," "The damsel in distress." Victims harbor a belief that they are unable to care for themselves. They feed the self-esteem needs of a Rescuer by telling them how much they need and appreciate them in order to keep the Rescuer taking care of them. Victims feel victimized, oppressed, hopeless, helpless, and ashamed. They often complain of depression or appear depressed due to the apparent hopelessness and helplessness of their position. They deny responsibility for their lives and deny having the power to change it. Being the Victim allows them to deny responsibility for failure or avoid even trying.

The Rescuer often believes that their own needs are not important and that they are sacrificing themselves for others. They believe that their only value is through helping others. You often see Rescuers in the roles of social worker, nurse, political activist as well as church volunteers and staff. When a Rescuer subjugates their own needs in excess of their capabilities, you will see burnout and resentment toward those they are rescuing. Rescuers often feel manipulated, used and unappreciated by those they are rescuing.

The Persecutor believes "It's all your fault." Known as the "villain" or "bad guy," Persecutors typically blame the Victims for being dependent and blame the Rescuers for enabling. They do this without providing any constructive solutions to the problem. The Persecutor role often origi-nates in shame. They feel and fear their own inadequacies and build themselves up by tearing others down. They compensate for their own flaws by focusing on those of others. They often try to reform others by guilt, shame, or force. Both Rescuers and Persecutors need a Victim in order to feel superior. Persecutors literally "blame the victim" by saying things like, "they deserved it" or "that's what you get."

The Family Roles

The Hero or "The Responsible One" tends to be successful in school, work or relationships outside of the family. They are reliable, organized, strong leadership skills, assertive, decisive, they are initiators, self-disciplined and goal oriented individuals. The heroes tend to struggle with

132

perfectionism, listening to others or relaxing. They lack spontaneity, being flexible, asking for help. They also have a strong fear of making mistakes and a strong need to be in control. The core beliefs that drive their present behaviors may include: "If I don't do it, no one will;" or "If I don't do this, something bad will happen, or things will get worse." As adults, Heroes may struggle with anxiety and depression symptoms.

The Placater or "People Pleasers" are caring, compassionate, empathic, good listeners and are giving to others. They tend to volunteer in community programs and work in social service occupations. The Placater tends to struggle with saying "No" to others, receiving praise or compliments, they will deny their own needs, and they will tolerant abuse and other inappropriate behaviors from others. Placaters frequently fear conflict and are often anxious and carry false guilt (not meeting self-imposed standards). The core beliefs that drive their present behaviors may include: "If I am nice, people will like me;" "If I focus on someone else, the focus won't be on me and that is good;" or "If I take care of you, you won't leave me or reject me." As adults, Placaters often express shaming attitudes, behaviors; they have a victimization mentality or play the martyr role ("look what I did for you and you treat me this way") they tend to use the "guilt trip" as a manipulative tool. The Placaters also struggle with depression or anxiety disorders.

The Scapegoat, "Addict" or "Problem Child" are creative, humorous and charismatic individuals. They gravitate toward creative occupations such as actors, musicians designers, etc. These individuals struggle to express emotions appropriately; they are often self-destructive, irresponsible, poor anger management, high school dropouts, underachievers and defiant/rebellious toward authority or to those who symbolize boundaries and limits. The core beliefs that drive their present behaviors may include: "If I scream loudly enough, someone may notice me;" or "I'll take what I want, no one is going to give me anything." As an adult, the Scapegoat shows shame, low esteem, rage, addictions, and procrastination.

The Lost Child or "Adjuster" is independent, easy going and quiet. They are flexible or have a "whatever" attitude. They follow easy and rarely question whose is charge. The Lost Child lack the ability to take the initiative, make decisions, perceiving choices and options. They are ignored and forgotten (which is in part what they want in order to not be hurt by others, unfortunately, it also maintains their feelings of being neglected and rejected). The core beliefs that drive their present behaviors may include: "If I don't get emotionally involved, I won't get hurt;" "I can't make a difference anyway;" "It is best not to draw attention to myself." As an Adult, the Lost Child tends to show shaming behaviors with procrastination, and have a victimized mentality.

The Mascot, "Distractor" or "Comedian" often displays a sense of humor; they are flexible and accommodating and are, able to relieve the stress and pain of uncomfortable situations. However, the Mascot is attention seekers, they will use humor to distract from issues that are necessary to address, and they can be immature and often use humor at inappropriate times. They lack focus and decision making ability. The core beliefs that drive their present behaviors include: "If I make people laugh, there is no pain;" "I am worthless;" or "If others knew me they would not like me." As an adult, Mascots may display anxiety, depression and struggle with addiction.

134

Appendix D

Core Belief Exercise

Instructions: Below and on the next page are some common core beliefs. On a separate sheet of paper; write the core belief(s) that you identify with. Describe the situation, person, or event that triggers that belief. *Example:* "I feel <u>I am unacceptable</u> when I am in the same room as my parents." ***Take your time!***

If others knew me they would not like me

I am unlovable I am unacceptable I am not special

I don't matter I am unworthy I am a mistake

I am mistrusting of others

I don't belong I don't fit in anywhere

I don't deserve to be happy

I'm not valuable

I am useless I am inadequate

I am crazy

I'm dirty

I am no good to anyone

Others will not meet my needs

I can't change

I am unwanted

I am not good enough

I am not good enough

I am inferior to others

I am worthless

I am afraid

I am defective

I am helpless

I am stupid

I am alone

I am bad

I often doubt myself

I need to be in control

I am hopeless

I am a failure

I am not whole

I am awkward

I am ugly

It's my fault

I am guilty

I am flawed

I can't be me around others

List the top three most impactful core beliefs:

1.

2.

3.

Now, from the top three chose the single most impactful core beliefs.

1.

Explain why this particular core belief is so influential to you?

_____

_____

_____

_____

_____

_____

_____

_____

Bibliography

Bradshaw, John. *The Family: A Revolutionary Way of Self-Discovery.* Deerfield Beach, Florida: Health Communication, Inc Publishing, 1998.

Carr, Nicholas (2008), "Is Google Making Us Stupid?" From http://www.theatlantic.com/magazine/archive/2008/07/is-google-making-us-stupid/6868. Retrieved on 6/26/2012, 2008.

Christ-Life. Net: "SATAN'S PLAN: Why We So Often Fail to Live Life More Abundantly." from: http://www.christ-life.net/prod02.htm. Retrieved on 9/7/2011.

Ekman, Paul Ph.D. *Emotions Revealed: Recognizing Faces and Feelings to Improve Communication and Emotional Life.* Second Edition. New York: Henry Holt and Company Publishing, 2003.

Firestone, W. Robert, Ph.D and Catlett, Joyce, MA (1986). *The Fantasy Bond: Structure of Psychological Defenses.* Washington, DC: American Psychological Association, 1986.

Ford, Charles, M.D. (1999), *Lies, Lies, Lies : The Psychology of Deceit.*, Arlington, VA: American Psychiatric Publishing, 1999.

Freyd, Jennifer, Ph.D. "Betrayal Trauma: Traumatic Amnesia as an Adaptive Response to Childhood Abuse." *Journal of Ethics & Behavior.* no 4:4 . Pages 307-329. 1994.

Hegstrom, Paul. *Broken Children, Grown-Up Pain, Understanding the Effects of Your Wounded Past,* Kansas, MO: Beacon Hill Press, 2001.

Life Application Study Bible. New International Version Bible. Grand Rapids, Michigan: Tyndale House Publishers, Inc. Wheaton, Illinois and Zondervan Publishing House, 1988.

Ornish, Dean, M.D. Love & Survival: The Scientific Basis for the Healing Power of Intimacy. New York: HarperCollins Publishing, 1998.

Schacter, Daniel, Ph.D. *The Seven Sins of Memory: How the Mind Forgets and Remembers.* Washington, DC.: American Psychological Association, 2001.

Steiner, Claude, Phd. *Emotional Literacy; Intelligence with a Heart.* Avon Books, 2002.

Whitfield, Charles, M.D. *Memory and Abuse: Remembering and Healing the Effects of Trauma.* Deerfield Beach, FL: Health Communication Publishing Inc.,1995.

About the Author

Edward Clark is a Licensed Professional Counselor, a state of Georgia Board Certified Clinical Advanced Alcohol and Drug Counselor, and an Internationally Certified Advanced Alcohol and Drug Counselor. He received his Master's degree in Christian counseling from Liberty University in Lynchburg, Virginia, and his Bachelor's degree in Criminal justice from National University in San Diego, California. He has twelve years of law enforcement experience, retiring in 2001. He has been a guest speaker on WAOK talk radio in Atlanta. Currently, he is in private practice in Cumming, Georgia, as well as providing consulting for recovery organizations, and acts as a speaker at various therapeutic seminars and workshops. He has been married for thirteen years and has two children.

For additional information, lectures, and workshop presentations, contact the author at:
www.lifefocus.biz

Or email:
ed@lifefocus.biz